More Praise for *Co-Active Leadership*

"You should get this book, read it, and do what it says. Karen and Henry wrote the book on coaching, and this current work extends their thinking and research into leadership. Great leaders are almost always great coaches, so this is a chance to learn from the masters."

—**Dave Logan, *New York Times* bestselling coauthor of *Tribal Leadership* and *The Three Laws of Performance* and faculty member, USC Marshall School of Business**

"Karen Kimsey-House and Henry Kimsey-House are rooted in a new and profound understanding of creativity in the universe. In brain science, cellular biology, ecosystem dynamics, and evolutionary cosmology, scientists are replacing the model of top-down control with a model of collaborative synergies. We have come to realize the way in which each individual carries a dimension of the whole system. There is no 'Star CEO' directing activities in a star; rather, the organizing intelligence of the star comes from the synergistic interactions within the entire community of atoms. *Co-Active Leadership* shows each of us how to move into this form of consciousness and pass through the gateway to our unique role in this historic shift from the modern industrial society to an integral civilization."

—**Brian Thomas Swimme, Professor, California Institute of Integral Studies; author of *The Hidden Heart of the Cosmos* and *The Universe Is a Green Dragon*; and creator of *Canticle to the Cosmos, Earth's Imagination,* and *The Powers of the Universe***

"The Co-Active Leadership Model has been a powerful tool in the transformation of our organization from a more traditional structure to one of shared leadership where everyone feels a sense of responsibility for the whole. It's been a remarkable shift, and I would recommend this book highly to anyone seeking to enhance participation, unleash creativity, and foster organizational change."

—**Bill Twist, cofounder and CEO, Pachamama Alliance**

"*Co-Active Leadership* is a groundbreaking book that cuts to the chase of what leadership really means in action! Clearly written with practical anecdotes, this is a must-read for anyone seeking to be a true leader."

—**Adrian Hayes, world-record-breaking adventurer, speaker, and leadership coach**

"I believe that everyone has the capacity to lead, and this book could not say it any better! What a gift for anyone thinking about leadership. This book will help transform your approach to leadership as well as provide an excellent resource on Co-Active Leadership."

—**HRH Princess Noor bint Asem, Hashemite Kingdom of Jordan, Co-Active Coach**

Co-Active Leadership

AUTHORS OF THE INTERNATIONAL BEST SELLER

Co-Active Coaching

CO-ACTIVE
LEADERSHIP
FIVE WAYS TO LEAD

Karen and Henry Kimsey-House

BK

Berrett–Koehler Publishers, Inc.
a BK Business book

BERRETT-KOEHLER PUBLISHERS, INC.
1333 Broadway, Suite 1000, Oakland, CA 94612-1921
Tel: (510) 817-2277   Fax: (510) 817-2278   www.bkconnection.com

ORDERING INFORMATION
QUANTITY SALES. Special discounts are available on quantity purchases by corporations, associations, and others. For details, contact the "Special Sales Department" at the Berrett-Koehler address above.

INDIVIDUAL SALES. Berrett-Koehler publications are available through most bookstores. They can also be ordered directly from Berrett-Koehler:
Tel: (800) 929-2929; Fax: (802) 864-7626; www.bkconnection.com

ORDERS FOR COLLEGE TEXTBOOK/COURSE ADOPTION USE. Please contact Berrett-Koehler:
Tel: (800) 929-2929; Fax: (802) 864-7626.

ORDERS BY U.S. TRADE BOOKSTORES AND WHOLESALERS. Please contact Ingram Publisher Services, Tel: (800) 509-4887; Fax: (800) 838-1149; E-mail: customer.service@ ingrampublisherservices.com; or visit www.ingrampublisherservices.com/Ordering for details about electronic ordering.

Berrett-Koehler and the BK logo are registered trademarks of Berrett-Koehler Publishers, Inc.

PRINTED IN THE UNITED STATES OF AMERICA

Berrett-Koehler books are printed on long-lasting acid-free paper. When it is available, we choose paper that has been manufactured by environmentally responsible processes. These may include using trees grown in sustainable forests, incorporating rec ycled paper, minimizing chlorine in bleaching, or recycling the energy produced at the paper mill.

LIBRARY OF CONGRESS CATALOGING-IN-PUBLICATION DATA
Kimsey-House, Karen.
Co-active leadership : five ways to lead / Karen and Henry
Kimsey-House. – First Edition.
    pages cm
Includes bibliographical references and index.
ISBN 978-1-62656-456-5 (pbk.)
1. Self-actualization (Psychology) 2. Mentoring. 3. Motivation
(Psychology) 4. Leadership–Psychological aspects. I. Kimsey-House,
Henry, 1953– II. Title.
BF637.S4K5457 2015
158'.4–dc23
                                2015012402

FIRST EDITION
20 19 18 17 16 15   10 9 8 7 6 5 4 3 2 1

INTERIOR DESIGN: VJB/Scribe   COVER DESIGN: Nicole Hayward
EDIT: Elissa Rabellino   PROOFREAD: Henrietta Bensussen
INDEX: Paula C. Durbin-Westby   PRODUCTION SERVICE: Linda Jupiter Productions

Dedicated to the Co-Active Leaders who have touched
our lives and the Co-Active Leaders yet to come

Contents

Preface

Co-Active Leadership: Five Ways to Lead offers a deeply collaborative approach to leadership, expanding beyond top-down, one-dimensional leadership models to alternatives that harness the possibility of many rather than relying on the power of one.

Co-Active Leadership is based on a few simple and somewhat radical themes, the first being that leadership needs to be approached in a multidimensional way to include a range of styles and approaches. This more inclusive understanding of leadership fosters connection and allows people to live and work together with shared ownership of whatever is being generated. The second theme of this book is that everyone is a leader regardless of role or title by choosing any one of five different ways to lead: Leader Within, Leader in Front, Leader Behind, Leader Beside, and Leader in the Field.

The Co-Active Leadership Model evolved from countless interactive conversations with different members of our worldwide Co-Active community (www.coactive.com). Our faculty, staff, international partners, students, individual clients, and corporate customers have all contributed immensely to the development of this model. The concepts that support the model, however, are rooted in our work in coaching and leadership development over the past twenty-plus years.

We wrote Co-Active Leadership to offer this new model of leadership as a choice available to anyone. In other words, we wrote this book for the dynamic and creative leader that lies within you, our reader. Reading this book can be transformative, or it can just be an intellectual exercise. The key is your willingness to let go of what you believe leadership to be and to hold it in a completely new context that can include everyone, most particularly *you*.

As you read *Co-Active Leadership*, we invite you to view each chapter as an invitation to reclaim different aspects of the compassionate, connected, creative leader within you. The first chapter, "A New Leadership Story," provides an overview of the principles of Co-Active Leadership. Chapter 2 outlines the Co-Active Leadership Model. Chapters 3 through 7 explore each aspect of the model more fully. The eighth chapter, "The Dance of the Dimensions," provides several examples of how people are using the Co-Active Leadership Model with their teams, clients, organizations, and families. Our final chapter, "The Good Life," is an expression of the larger context of Co-Active Leadership. The stories we share are from our own experience or the experience of our students and clients. When others were involved, we have changed the names of the characters to protect confidentiality.

If we are going to overcome the daunting challenges of our time, we must learn how to collaborate together in new ways that allow us to access the diverse talent and abilities of many. We hope that *Co-Active Leadership* will prove to be both a practical guide and an inspiring journey for you and that it will support you in generating an experience of wholeness and success in your work and in your world.

A New Leadership Story

On October 17, 1989, the workday in San Francisco was just coming to a close. South of the city in Candlestick Park, thousands had gathered to watch game three of the World Series. At 5:04 p.m., the Loma Prieta earthquake struck, shaking the earth, shattering windows, knocking down buildings and overpasses, and kicking up huge clouds of dust. Electricity was out throughout the San Francisco Bay Area, and it was difficult to find out what had really happened. People flooded out of the downtown Financial District, intending to walk home or make their way through a tangle of automobiles and cable cars, as all the traffic lights were out.

At Kearny and Pine, however, traffic was flowing freely. A homeless man, well known for his presence on one of the corners of this particular intersection, was directing traffic. He had placed himself in the center of the intersection and was managing the flow with great care and panache. He stood tall as he waved cars forward from one direction and held his hand up firmly as he instructed others to stop and wait. Attorneys, stockbrokers, and other highly paid executives all followed his direction without question. People who just the day before had walked by the homeless man without a second glance now honked, waved, and blew him kisses.

No one had told the homeless fellow that he was the one to step up and lead. He didn't need to wait for the authorities to arrive and give him a title. He just saw the need and decided that he was the man for the job. Those who were following his directions did not need to see a résumé to determine whether he had the requisite training. They immediately became dedicated co-leaders, eager to serve and support in whatever way they could.

Amid the chaos and disruption of the earthquake, at the intersection of Kearny and Pine, leadership was flowing freely. There were no fancy titles and no one was elected. People did not give a great deal of thought to what was in it for them or if they were interested in being responsible. They just acted from their own humanity and heart, providing whatever was needed in the moment in a variety of different ways.

Our current view of leadership tends to be one-dimensional, with leadership being the responsibility of one or two people at the top. As the story above demonstrates, this viewpoint is not particularly accurate.

In reality, leadership is multidimensional. In any project or community there are many different leaders, each leading in different ways, with people changing roles fluidly. In any given day, each of us moves through a range of different leadership dimensions. We are all leaders in one way or another, and when we choose to be responsible for what is happening around us, we are able to work together in a way that includes and utilizes the unique talents of everyone.

Take our friend John, who is on his way to work as a legal secretary at a widely respected law firm. John is grateful for his life. While he understands that he is not perfect by a long shot, he does his best to live with integrity. He began the day as he does most others, with a short meditation and some reading to connect to his purpose and values. He leaves his apartment feeling present, alive, and ready to meet the day.

As John walks along, he sees a small child totter out into a busy roadway. Without a moment's hesitation, he leaps forward and snatches the child back to safety, taking a few extra moments to ensure that the child is returned to the care of his grateful parents.

Enjoying the spring sunshine, John mulls over a project that has become stalled. What's the big picture? he wonders. What is bogging things down? He senses that there are some things that are unspoken among the team members and badly need to be said. He makes a mental note to encourage a deeper conversation at the next team meeting.

Once at work, John leaves a sticky note on his boss's desk. His boss is up for a big promotion, and John wants to let her know that he's rooting for her and believes in her 100 percent.

In the kitchen, John runs into his co-worker Shayna. They are co-leading a game night for the staff the following evening, and they take a moment to work out a few of the details.

John has just been a leader in five different ways, and his workday hasn't even officially begun!

The purpose of this book is to offer a simple model of multi-dimensional leadership that can by accessed by anyone to generate more aliveness and ownership of one's world and one's life.

In this more accurate multidimensional view of leadership, everyone has the capacity to be a leader by moving fluidly through five different dimensions of leadership as the circumstances and the situation require. These dimensions are Leader Within, Leader in Front, Leader Behind, Leader Beside, and Leader in the Field.

For each dimension, the key to success is balancing our essence and our action, our being and our doing. This is the foundation of Co-Active Leadership.

What Is Co-Active?

At its most basic, *Co-Active* means simply being in action . . . together. Or perhaps it might be more appropriate to say being together . . . in action.

The *co* represents the relational and receptive aspects of our world. The *active* follows and represents the action-oriented aspects.

As the pace of our lives has quickened, we have become increasingly action oriented and results driven. It seems expedient to dispense with all the "soft" stuff of being and just push to get the job done that is right in front of us. Unfortunately, this leaves us feeling disconnected and desperate for meaning and belonging. We wind up with what we might call "the hamster wheel" experience of life as we run around alone in circles desperately trying to get things done, only to find ourselves right back where we started.

This is why it is so important to begin with the *co*. Action arising from this place of being and receptivity is whole and integrated rather than disconnected and driven. In order for us to experience life as whole, action must be grounded in being and our sense of connection to a larger wholeness. When the *co* and the *active* go together, the action of our life is nourishing and fulfilling.

Karen, one of the authors of this book, was teased by her colleagues because they saw her smiling as she responded to emails. When asked why she was smiling, Karen responded, "Well, I'm thinking about the people who will be reading this e-mail and the things I enjoy about them. I imagine the relationship between us, and it makes me smile." Thus a task that could be dreary and isolating became joyful because it held a balance of both *co* and *active*, even though Karen was physically alone.

The hyphen in Co-Active is very important because it holds both the interrelatedness and the balance between *co* and *active*.

The hyphen represents the paradox of "both and" rather than "either/or."

Generally, we tend to live in an either/or world. Either we can be effective and get the job done, or we can care for the people in our lives. Either we can take a break and attend to our well-being, or we can work hard and accomplish things.

Yet, everything in our natural world teaches us that these two energies of *co* and *active* weave together in every moment. So, like the yin and yang of ancient Chinese Taoist philosophy, *co* and *active* dance together to create wholeness and balance.

Everyone Is a Leader

In this multidimensional model of leadership, everyone has within them the capacity to lead, and any organization or community is most dynamic, most alive, and most productive when there is a commitment to leadership at every level. We all share full responsibility for the experience we generate, and our sense of personal power and fulfillment is directly commensurate with the level of ownership we are able to take for what happens to and around us.

We don't have much to say about the challenges, hardships, and disasters (natural and otherwise) that befall us. This is the stuff that our lives are made of. However, we do have everything to say about how we engage and who we *are* in the events of our lives, about whether we offer ourselves or put our heads in the sand, about whether we seek to serve or give way to blame. We get to choose whether we will take responsibility for the world we are creating.

In this way, we have a kind of power that cannot be given to us and therefore cannot be taken away. Life is no longer just happening to us–we are co-creators and we share in the challenge and joy of shaping our world to reflect our own values and purpose.

We Create Our World.
Together.
Every Day.

Everyone has the capacity to contribute and to choose responsibility. Everyone has the capacity to lead. Leadership is a choice, and it begins with one's willingness to be responsible for what is happening in one's world.

A New Definition of Leadership

In order to set leadership free from a one-dimensional view, we would offer that rather than being defined by position or title, *leaders are those who are responsible for their world.*

What does it mean to be responsible? The word *responsibility* is often associated with burden, with something that is mandated. The dictionary defines responsibility as "the state or fact of having a duty to deal with something" and "the state or fact of being accountable or to blame for something." Responsibility feels heavy, significant, dutiful, and perhaps a bit scary.

We'd like to offer a more expansive definition of responsibility. What if responsibility existed outside of the burden of the task, of getting the job done? What if we interpreted responsibility as a choice rather than a burden? What if the choice of responsibility generated a context of ownership and self-authorship beyond the immediate task at hand? In this new context, responsibility becomes generative and nourishing rather than weighty and burdensome.

As we choose responsibility, we immediately have more free-dom and creativity. We are able to shift from being a passenger with things happening to us and instead be open to the challenges of our lives and allow them to shape and grow us. We are able to break free from our ego's fears and need for approval and instead meet our world with power and with love. Life is just more *fun* when we are choosing to be responsible. We experience our life as an unfolding adventure rather than something to be endured. The difference is as dramatic as the difference between eating the white pith of an orange and savoring a burst of the sweet juice.

In Co-Active Leadership, responsibility has two important parts. The first part is to be response-able: able to respond. In other words, we must have the awareness to notice what is needed in the moment and the agility to respond from a wide palette of creative choices rather than from an entrenched system of patterned and predict-able reactions. This is the *co* of responsibility.

The *active* aspect of responsibility entails choosing to be respon-sible as cocreators of our lives and our world. The circumstances of life will come and go, from birth to death with the full range of human experience in between. These ups and downs are a given in our human journey.

However, we have everything to say about how we respond to these circumstances. We have the choice to react in a patterned way, blaming someone else for what is happening, or to *create* from those same circumstances, using whatever happens as an opportunity to evolve and grow ourselves and the people around us.

When we choose to be responsible and creative rather than reac-tive, we stop being victims of our lives. We cease to feel as if we are running down a hill after our life, trying to catch up. Instead, the choice of responsibility puts us squarely in the driver's seat of our life. We become coauthors and cocreators of our lives rather than merely passengers. Now we are aware and alert enough to respond to circumstances, and we have enough self-authority to be creative and expand our range by consciously choosing to act from a full menu of options.

Leadership development, then, becomes about growing the size of the world for which one is able to be responsible. Sometimes this area is very small. Some people are not able to be responsible even for the world of themselves, and they move through life unconsciously, bumping into different people and experiences without self-awareness.

This understandably creates concern about the concept of anyone being capable of choosing leadership. What about the people who *are* unconscious, who don't want to be responsible and choose instead to hide from responsibility? Don't these people have to be prodded and controlled and told what to do?

And what about all those other people who are selfish and dominating and don't care at all about other people? Don't we need to guard against these people? How can we possibly hold these people as capable of leadership? Doesn't that just lower the bar and weaken the power of leadership for everyone else?

We would maintain that the capacity to grow both our self-awareness and our ability to be responsible is available to anyone. It's important to be present with people wherever they are (*co*) and at the same time provide them with opportunities to choose responsibility and act powerfully (*active*). When we adopt a Co-Active framework for leadership, we are available to be receptive to people while at the same time holding them accountable for their actions.

In our experience, people generally want to do well. The more we look for a demonstration of responsibility, the more we will find it. If you believe that people are broken and in need of fixing, they will likely perform to your expectations. If you view people as generally creative and resourceful, it's more likely that you will find those qualities in others. As we create our world together, every day, it's important to pay attention to where we are placing our attention. So often, people feel powerless and ineffective because they have been told that they are wrong and that they don't have what it takes to lead effectively.

For several years, Karen had the opportunity to work with inmates of several prisons. This was a real gift, as it taught her a great deal about how people are trained from a very early age to view themselves as unworthy. The men that Karen worked with knew for certain that they were not leaders. They had begun life as "problem children." As teenagers, they graduated to being "juvenile delinquents," and as adults, they moved on to be criminals and convicts. Their view of themselves as defective had been consistently reinforced for much of their lives.

Karen and her co-leaders remained committed to viewing these men as valuable human beings who were capable of goodness and wholeness. While firmly believing that they should be held accountable for their *actions* and for the crimes that they had committed, Karen and her co-leaders also maintained that they were whole and resourceful human beings, capable of learning and responsibility and worthy of respect and love.

Over time, the men began to turn toward this positive regard like sunflowers toward the sun. Many began to change the way they dressed and talked. Others reached out to repair relationships with family members and loved ones. Some began to talk about how they could make a difference in the world and how they might be able to prevent others from making the kinds of choices that had cost them so much.

Not all the men opened up. For some, that creative leader within was buried so deeply that it might never see the light of day. Some remained inaccessible, lost in a haze of drugs or alcohol or mental illness.

Still, there was a considerable change in many of the men, and for Karen it fortified the certainty that we don't really know what has happened to people and why they act as they do. While people must be held to account for their actions, they are still human beings worthy of respect and even love.

If we can respect the being of people (*co*) while at the same time enforcing accountability for action (*active*), and if we can support a multidimensional understanding of leadership, all kinds of change become possible.

2

The Co-Active Leadership Model

One-dimensional models of leadership do not have the range to celebrate and honor different expressions of leadership. To be truly effective, communities–whether in the family or in the workplace–need a model that is multidimensional and inclusive. This allows leadership to be a flexible system in which everyone can assume leadership regardless of his or her role or title and move fluidly through different dimensions of leadership, depending on the needs of the moment.

Multidimensionality and agility allow us to access a broader range of resources from a number of powerful leaders, each taking responsibility in a different way. Collaborative solutions emerge that would not have been available from one-dimensional, hierarchical leadership structures in which important considerations are often overlooked.

The Co-Active Leadership Model offers five different dimensions, five different ways to lead. Though it is useful to pull the different dimensions apart for the sake of learning and practice, the dimensions of the Co-Active Leadership Model are designed to work together. Everyone, at different times, plays all five roles, shifting from dimension to dimension as the circumstances and the needs of the moment require.

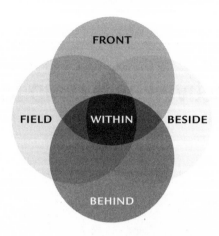

The Co-Active Leadership Model

When Co-Active Leadership is really working, leadership is shared at every level in a system, be it an organization, a family system, or some other kind of community. While there are various roles and responsibilities, everyone involved feels committed and engaged because they understand that they have an important contribution to make to the success of the whole.

It's normal to find that we are more skillful and comfortable in one dimension than another. For example, some of us excel at Leader in Front and need to learn to give way to others from time to time. Others of us are extraordinary at Leader Behind and tend to shy away from the spotlight. As Co-Active leaders, we need practice all the dimensions of the model and learn to shift from one to the other nimbly.

Sometimes there is concern that with so many people contributing and participating, we won't be able to move forward effectively. We fear that there will be too much *co* and not enough *active*. It is important to remember that participation is not the same as agreement. It is entirely possible for a group of people to move forward quite effectively, aligned around a common vision and with considerable disagreement about the most effective action. When people are allowed to own responsibility for the decisions they make, they can seek advice and input from others while still making a considered decision that does not comply with everyone's opinion.

Leader Within lies at the center of the model and is formed by the overlap of the remaining four dimensions, which are Leader in Front, Leader Behind, Leader Beside, and Leader in the Field. This is because the dimension of Leader Within is unique and also present in all the other dimensions.

What follows is a brief description of the dimensions of Co-Active Leadership. In the following chapters, we'll be illustrating each dimension more fully and offer examples of how the dimension might be utilized.

Co-Active Leader Within:
Self-Acceptance and Self-Authority

In the Co-Active Leader Within dimension, we are striving to be our best self every day and to follow Mahatma Gandhi's instruction "Be the change that you wish to see in the world."[1] Co-Active Leaders Within take responsibility for their world by accepting themselves fully (*co*) and living their lives with integrity in accordance with their personal values (*active*).

When we are able to choose our own humanity with all of its brilliance and imperfection, we can let go of trying to fix ourselves and instead reach to expand and grow so that we both live our life more fully and offer more to our world.

In this dimension, we know that we are enough and that simply living our life with openheartedness and integrity will suffice.

Co-Active Leader in Front:
Connection and Direction

When we think of leadership, we usually think of Leader in Front. Being a Co-Active Leader in Front, however, is not about being the boss and telling everyone what to do.

Co-Active Leaders in Front foster connection with the people who are following them (*co*) and stand firmly for a clear direction and purpose (*active*).

When a Leader in Front is Co-Active, people feel inspired, engaged, and clear. They are able to give their best because they all know that they are important and valuable.

As Co-Active Leaders in Front, we can let go of figuring out everything on our own because we understand that we need other people's input to make our vision real.

Most of all, in the dimension of Co-Active Leader in Front, we are not trapped by ego or defined by our role. While we are willing to be the one in front and will do our best to point the way, we also know when to sit down and make room for other people's creativity and talent.

Co-Active Leader Behind:
Serving and Coaching

The essence of Co-Active Leader Behind is service to others. Rather than trying to look good or get ahead, Co-Active Leaders Behind focus on providing whatever is needed and, through openhearted and enthusiastic participation, advance the action in a way that holds everyone together. They are, therefore, the backbone of any organization or undertaking.

Co-Active Leaders Behind are committed to empowering and calling forth the brilliance of other people by believing in them and coaching them through deep listening, powerful questions, and acknowledgment.

It is important to note that Co-Active Leader Behind is not about deferring or letting go. Co-Active Leaders Behind understand that we all must work together, and they seek to provide whatever is needed for the whole. In this dimension, we know that we matter and are clear that our wholehearted participation is a critical part of any endeavor.

Co-Active Leader Beside: Partnership and Synergy

Most of the time, co-leading consists of dividing responsibilities and taking turns. Co-Active Leader Beside is a partnership between two people in which both people are 100 percent responsible for every part of the initiative.

Co-Active Leaders Beside take responsibility for their world by consciously designing their partnership around a shared vision and intention (*co*) and leveraging each other's strengths so that a remarkable synergy occurs with the whole being that is greater than the sum of the parts (*active*).

Co-Active Leaders Beside are committed to leaning into their co-leader 100 percent, balancing openness and curiosity about the other person with a commitment to stand fully in their own authority. In the dimension of Co-Active Leader Beside, we can disagree with each other in a way that is dynamic and productive because we are both committed to something larger than being right about our own point of view.

Co-Active Leader in the Field:
Intuition and Innovation

Co-Active Leader in the Field is not about leading a project, a team, or even an organization. Instead, Co-Active Leader in the Field is about noticing and taking responsibility for our impact in and on our world. If, as we said in chapter 1, leaders are those who are responsible for their world, the dimension of Co-Active Leader in the Field connects us to a global sense of the world we are creating.

In the dimension of Co-Active Leader in the Field, we slow down and expand our sensory awareness so that we can access our imagination, intuition, and insight (*co*), and have the courage and commitment to act on what we sense in a way that is innovative and new (*active*).

When we slow down and open up our senses, new understanding comes that we just can't access from the hustle of our daily routines. We are able to see the big picture and discover patterns and cycles that can lead us to new insight and innovation.

Co-Active Leaders in the Field take responsibility for their world by slowing down and observing the deeper implications of what is happening, and by trusting their instinct and intuition beyond what is known and can be proved.

Going Deeper into the Model

In the next chapters, we will open up the Co-Active Leadership Model so that we can explore each of the dimensions more fully.

In chapter 8, "The Dance of the Dimensions," we'll put the model back together again, providing several examples of how people are using it in their work with themselves and with their organizations, teams, students, and families.

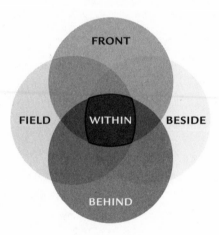

3

Co-Active Leader Within

Many years ago, Karen was planting a summer garden with her 6-year-old niece, Christin. They began with the marigolds, tucking the sharp seeds into the rich brown soil. Karen's job was to plant the seeds and make sure that the rows were straight. Christin was to come along behind her, placing the seed packet with its picture of bright orange flowers onto a Popsicle stick at the end of each row. After a time, Karen noticed that Christin had placed the pictures on the seed packets inward, facing toward the newly planted marigolds. "Christin," she said, "honey, you need to turn the picture around so that we can see what we've planted when we look out at our garden." "Oh no, Auntie K," Christin said solemnly. "The marigolds need to see the picture so that they will know what they are supposed to look like when they grow up."

While this little story is charming, it is also rather sad because it illustrates, all too clearly, how we are taught from an early age to look outside ourselves for who we are supposed to be and how we are supposed to act.

Actually, in a one-dimensional, top-down leadership system, it is essential that the voice of our self-authority be oppressed so that we can be easily controlled and "managed." We are taught to live from the outside in, gathering the images that show us how we should look and act. In school, we are taught how to behave, standing in rows with our hands by our sides and waiting until it is our turn. Through countless messages we see every day, we are taught that we are not really good enough and therefore need to buy an endless array of products to try to close the gap. As adults, we are controlled through comparison and positioning so that we become oppressed, reactionary beings rather than authors of our own realities.

Of course, the images that our environment reflects back to us are often not very realistic or even attainable. This leaves us striving for some unreachable version of ourselves that will be acceptable to others. Sadly, we always fall short. We are always too *something* . . . too short, too tall, too hairy, too bald, too soft-spoken, or too bossy for some group of people. Yet so many of us continue to try to fit the expansiveness of our being into a neat and tailored version of ourselves that we hope will be pleasing to the world.

We come to believe that we create value by what we do rather than by who we are, so we strive to prove our worth by performing well. This does not leave much room for failure, for our own humanity and imperfection. While there is nothing wrong with working hard or challenging ourselves to reach for the stars, when these actions stem from misguided attempts to prove our worth in an absence of self-acceptance, they will always leave us wanting.

What Is Co-Active Leader Within?

The dimension of Co-Active Leader Within begins with the choice to live one's life from the inside out rather than the outside in. This is a radical and deeply transformative shift. Everything changes when we finally cast off the shackles of striving for approval and acceptance outside of our own skin and instead decide that we are in fact good enough–that there is nothing we need to do to earn acceptance, approval, or love.

When we choose ourselves as we are, including both our shadow and our light, we can move beyond our ego's need for perfection and embrace the ongoing adventure of life. We are able to claim authorship of our own life and live with integrity according to our own internal compass, guided by our purpose and values. This self-acceptance and self-authority are the *co* and the *active* of Co-Active Leader Within.

We tend to think of leadership as externally focused on the objective or the goal rather than beginning with the truth of our own hearts. In reality, the self is the only place to begin. If we are not at home within ourselves, it is difficult to make grounded, conscious choices. When we are unfamiliar with the diverse terrain of our own internal landscape, our options will be fairly limited and one-dimensional.

Co-Active Leaders Within lead by living their lives with integrity and modeling self-acceptance and self-authority. Of course, from time to time we will stumble. Failure and recovery are important parts of development and growth, and if we demand perfection, our lives will become sanctimonious and lifeless. It is a good idea to hold our journey with compassion for our own humanity and a robust sense of humor.

Instead of being taught to look outward to an airbrushed and perfectly lit supermodel image of what we were supposed to look like, what if the marigold in us were taught to look inward toward the sun of our own beauty and magnificence? What if our roots were firmly planted in the rich soil of belonging and self-acceptance so that we were nourished by our uniqueness and secure in our place in the family of things? How might we grow and flourish?

What Is the *Co*?

Self-acceptance, the *co* aspect of Co-Active Leader Within, begins with being present to ourselves just as we are. We only have to practice being more present to be astonished by how often, in fact, we are not. Our minds do tend to wander a bit, quite often behaving like an unruly puppy that refuses to sit.

In our experience, learning how to be present is the journey of a lifetime. There's generally always room for improvement, and about the time we get all excited and impressed with how present we are, well, there you go . . . we've drifted away from the moment!

In our experience, gratitude for what currently exists makes presence more accessible. It's much easier to be present to the life that you *are* living than the one you wish you were living or think you *should* be living.

Gratitude is a simple practice, and yet it is one of the most healing things we know. We're not talking about abstract positive affirmations here. Sometimes it takes real dedication to find value in what is happening to us. Our human experience is filled with a wide range of experiences and challenges. The temptation to numb ourselves or to judge or blame others can be quite strong.

In Co-Active Leader Within, the challenges that present themselves along the journey of our life become opportunities to strengthen and grow rather than insufferable hardships that must be endured. This doesn't mean that we need to be happy or enlightened all the time. It just means that we understand that there is an opportunity in everything, and if we look for it, we will find it.

When we are able to celebrate the ups and downs of our life as they are happening, it becomes much easier to be comfortable inside our skin and embrace our own humanity with all of its beauty and imperfection. Once we can free ourselves from the tyranny of looking good, getting it right, and performing for others, we can settle into our own unique expression of self and learn and grow from whatever life offers us.

To truly develop as a Co-Active Leader Within, we must stop holding our imperfections as a problem in need of fixing and instead approach our own development with the understanding that every part of us is there for a reason. Everything we need is already within us, and our journey as a Co-Active Leader Within is a journey of reclaiming our true nature.

In our work over the past twenty-plus years, we have seen the strength and power of Co-Active Leader Within blossom and flourish once the context for personal development shifted from one of brokenness to one of wholeness and sufficiency.

To make this shift from brokenness to wholeness, we must be willing to let go of beliefs that no longer serve us. Sometimes it seems that it is just too hard to choose responsibility for the life we are creating. It's easier, we tell ourselves, to remain a bit numb, wrapping ourselves in a cloud of justifications. Sometimes it *feels* easier to live from old, life-diminishing beliefs . . . but is it really?

Recently we attended an outdoor program in the beautiful high desert of New Mexico. Part of the program focused on limiting beliefs and how we tend to drag them around behind us like a string of old rusty tin cans.

The facilitators began by dumping a bunch of rusty cans in the middle of our circle. Each can had a hole punched in the middle, and each person received six of the cans and a length of twine.

Our assignment was to spend the afternoon hiking across the land, looking enthusiastically for limiting beliefs that held us back from experiencing the magic and beauty of life. For the duration of the afternoon, we were to drag our tin cans behind us, tied to one ankle with twine.

Off we went with our tin cans clattering in our dust. Almost immediately, the cans got snagged in bushes and on rocks. After a time, many of us had added to our load as the cans picked up scoopfuls of dirt and pebbles and all kinds of sticks and twigs. Our strings kept breaking, requiring us to take repeated breaks in our journey to fashion all kinds of creative repairs.

As the afternoon progressed, it became completely clear to all of us how foolish it was to cling to these limiting beliefs. We were having a visceral experience of how much these beliefs slowed us down and held us back from where we wanted to go. We were shocked to discover how much time and energy we needed to spend caring for and maintaining them. The afternoon was hilarious and tragic at the same time.

We all have these kinds of beliefs that we drag around after us like rattling old tin cans, and we spend all manner of time validating, justifying, and caring for these beliefs. We cling to them, sometimes ferociously.

We've had clients staunchly defend their worthlessness, and when we attempted to champion them as leaders, they insisted that we did not know what we were talking about. Capable and talented? No, thank you. There were quite convinced that they were, in fact, terrible parents, lousy managers, worthless people, and most definitely, most certainly, *not* leaders.

It takes conscious choice to cut the twine that binds us to our limiting beliefs and holds us in a story of powerlessness. The reward on the other side of that choice is freedom and a new relationship with our own ability to be the author of our own lives.

What Is the *Active*?

Letting go of old limiting beliefs doesn't happen overnight, but it is work worth doing. We call it "cleaning out the basement." If held in a context of self-discovery, this work creates the raw materials to write the story of our life in whatever way is most nourishing. The circumstances do not need to change in order for our story to change from an endless tale of helplessness and despair to a hero's journey rich with appreciation, opportunity, and growth.

Self-authority is not a destination, not something we are permitted to claim only when we are good enough or enlightened enough. The journey of self-authority begins in the immediate moment with the decision to take responsibility for the authorship of one's own life.

We can't control (to any great extent) *what* happens in our lives. We do have complete authority over who we *are* and the story we tell ourselves about those events.

Two women are losing their father, their last surviving parent, to cancer. For Eloise, the journey is terrifying and overwhelming. Her life is so busy, packed with the demands of her job and the challenge of raising three children. She loves her father very much, but deep inside, she is so afraid of what is happening to him and to her. She is also angry. Why did this have to happen to her? Why did this have to happen to her father? She hates the loss of control and the sense that she is powerless to have things be different. She does her best to care for her father, but she finds it difficult to talk about what is happening inside her. He's so sick, and she doesn't want to bother him. When her father passes away, she feels a deep sadness and also a vast emptiness.

For Janis, the journey is one of heartbreak and transformation. She has a full life with a demanding job and the challenge of raising her three children, but she wants to spend as much time with her dad as possible, so she talks with people at work and in her family and enlists their support, asking them to take on some tasks that would normally fall to her. She and her dad face the journey together and talk often about what death means to each of them. When her father passes away, she feels a deep sadness and also tremendous gratitude for the gift of sharing this important passage with him.

The two stories feature the same situation. However, the experiences of the two women are completely different. This is what we mean when we say: We create our world. Together. Every day. Every moment of our lives is an opportunity to write or rewrite our story in a way that is nourishing and life affirming if we choose to do so.

Our sense of our life purpose and our understanding of our personal values and principles can guide us in creating a life story that is vibrant and fulfilling. While it is fine to pursue the external trappings of success, such as status and money, these things don't bring us a deeper sense of fulfillment. Understanding and articulating our life purpose can serve as a guide toward a greater expression of our Co-Active Leader Within, and that in turn generates meaning and a sense of connectedness in our lives.

Our life purpose is a path, not a destination. Like the North Star, our purpose helps us to steer a true course for the journey of our life. During our lives, we will find many different expressions of our life purpose. We will engage in different relationships, hold different jobs, and adopt different roles. While all these things are avenues through which to express our life purpose, that purpose transcends them all and weaves through the whole of our life. Whether or not we can articulate our life purpose, if we are truthful with ourselves, we generally have a sense of those life choices that are on purpose and those that are not.

Creating a life-purpose statement is like standing on the top of a tall hill: You can see the contribution you are here to make in a larger context. Finding and claiming a life purpose gives us a powerful sense of direction in our lives and provides a powerful compass for the Co-Active Leader Within.

Beginning to articulate one's life purpose is a process that takes time. The process can involve personal reflection, reading, keeping a journal, or working with a coach. Continuing to excavate and express our life purpose creates a context of meaning for our lives. We come to understand a little bit about the mystery of why we are here, in this life at this time. The more we explore, the more we understand.

Clarifying our personal values is another valuable tool for understanding what it means to live in integrity. Values are not morals or principles or standards of behavior. They are also not something we do or have. Values are intangible and personal. They are the qualities of a life lived fully from the inside out. By honoring our personal values, we live in integrity with *ourselves* first. This fosters a life of resonance and meaning. No one can tell us what should matter to us most—not our parents or our culture. These are things we must discover for ourselves.

The process of values clarification is about looking within and identifying what is truly most important and most resonant for us as a unique individual. One person might have a high value of serenity and choose to live in the country. Another might have a high value of excitement and choose the city life. While neither choice is right or wrong, it would be a mistake to switch them. Life would not be as fulfilling for the country dweller in the midst of a city, and the city person would become bored and restless living too far away from the bright lights of the city.

Again, the work of clarifying one's own values takes time and dedication. In a world of quick answers and ready information, people can be reluctant to take the time. However, while the process of values clarification does take time and commitment, it is time well spent. Once we have a clear sense of our own top values, they become a road map for living a life of fulfillment and integrity.

For example, if something is not going well at work, we can examine our values. Usually we will find that one of our values is being suppressed or not honored. If there is a challenge in a relationship in our personal lives, the same is true. It is difficult to walk our talk if we are not living in accordance with our top values.

When we live our lives from the internal compass of our life purpose and values, we lead by example through the integrity of our day-to-day activities, and our lives are a contribution to our world. We offer our whole and creative selves to our world, and our participation is nourishing.

If we offer a story of a broken and wounded self to others, we will need others to take care of us and to help us feel more whole. This is codependency, not contribution.

When we orient from a place of wholeness, we can express ourselves from a place of abundance and love because our expression comes from a desire to serve and contribute rather than a place of personal need.

This is the difference between being filled with self and being self-absorbed. When we are self-absorbed, we are trying to *get* what we need from the world around us so that we can feel whole. When we are filled with gratitude and the self-acceptance and self-authority of Co-Active Leader Within, that abundance overflows naturally and nourishes those around us.

This is what we mean when we say, "Leaders are those who are responsible for their world." When we do our own internal work and "clean out our basement," we bring wholeness to our world.

Notice that we did not mention perfection. Conflict still arises. Disagreement occurs. Sometimes there will be anger, disappointment, and hurt feelings. Confusion will erupt. Chaos will swirl. When held in a context of wholeness and connection, these occurrences become opportunities to expand and grow rather than overwhelming challenges to be avoided at all cost. Like the Cowardly Lion in *The Wizard of Oz*, we don't have to be afraid to go into the dark woods because we know we have the resiliency and courage to face whatever challenges are there.

In our experience, human beings share a powerful longing and desire to contribute to the world around them. We want to know that we made a difference in our time here on earth. Co-Active Leader Within is an opportunity to express that longing in every moment from a place of generosity and heart. We don't need to have the answers. We only need to live in integrity from our purpose and values and to ask ourselves what might be our most useful and life-affirming contribution in this moment.

What about the Hyphen?

As human beings, we are potential unfolding over the course of our lives rather than problems that need to be solved. In the place of *co*, of essence, there is absolutely nothing to do but live our lives fully.

At the same time, while there is nothing to fix or do, it is important to continually reach for an ever-expanding version of our self. So in Co-Active Leader Within, the interplay between doing and being is important because it helps us ground our action in essence and meaning, and it moves us forward into an ever more expansive expression of ourselves.

In this context, self-discovery becomes both an adventure and an act of service. We grow ourselves in order to be more useful to our world rather than in order to get ahead or make more money. We let go of the illusion that we need to *do* a lot of things in order to *have* a lot of things so that we can *be* happy and fulfilled. Instead, we *are* fulfilled, and from that we *do* things that bring us joy and fulfillment so that we *have* a life that is rich with learning, self-discovery, partnership, and love.

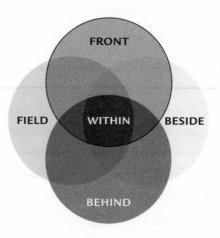

4

Co-Active Leader in Front

When we think about leaders and leadership, we usually think of some variation of Leader in Front. We have created myths, legends, and heroic stories about brilliant and inspiring leaders who have stepped out in front and said, "I see where we need to go. Follow me."

Co-Active Leader in Front, however, is not about being the boss and dominating everyone, ordering them around and telling them what to do. The difficulty with this kind of command-and-control, one-dimensional leadership is that it creates separation and distance.

In this one-dimensional approach, leadership becomes transactional rather than relational as those at the top do whatever is necessary to achieve the objective, to meet the numbers. It is unacceptable to stumble or fall. To be a successful leader, one must have ready answers and make crisp decisions. Failure is not an option.

Often, these leaders are isolated because they can't afford to get too close to the people who are following them, lest their authority be compromised. They are the ones who are responsible for making the big decisions, and while they might get input from others, they must make decisions on their own to avoid appearing weak or wishy-washy.

What Is Co-Active Leader in Front?

Co-Active Leaders in Front generate an experience of inclusion and connection with the people who are following them while at the same time articulating a clear direction and purpose.

Co-Active Leaders in Front are willing to step to the front because they hold a strong commitment to evoking the best for everyone within a context of vision and heart.

When there is no *co* in Leader in Front, what's missing is connection to people. When there is no *active*, people do not feel certain and clear. Great Co-Active Leaders in Front engage others in a way that is exciting and inspiring and act for the betterment and development of the people they are leading.

Our organizational world is filled with examples of what happens when the co is missing from Leader in Front. All the focus is on the task, and everyone keeps trying to figure out what "the boss" is after. No collaboration. No connection. Not much creativity either.

And then there's what we might call "faux co." We had an executive client who took a management workshop and learned that taking an interest in people improved productivity. The workshop had carefully compiled the statistics to prove this, along with 10 easy steps for taking an interest in others. Following the guideline "Take an interest in what people do outside of work," our hapless executive began calling his direct reports into his office every Monday morning and grilling them about what they had done over the weekend. Predictably, people were uncomfortable and suspicious.

Caring for and empowering other people just isn't a paint-by-numbers sort of thing. Co-Active Leader in Front takes heart and vulnerability as well as courage and commitment.

What Is the *Co*?

The *co* of Co-Active Leader in Front is about connection, engagement, and inclusion. As Patrick Lencioni states in his book *The Advantage*, "If people don't weigh in, they can't buy in."[2] Even if the direction that is ultimately taken is different than what they would have wanted, people will be able to engage and trust if they have been able to contribute through conversation and disagreement.

The best way for a Co-Active Leader in Front to generate connection and engagement is through dynamic and generative conversation. When we speak of conversation, we are not talking about meaningless platitudes or superficial chitchat. A real conversation has substance and depth.

The word *conversation* derives from the Latin for "to turn about with." What if every conversation were an opportunity to turn *with* someone *toward* something?

Any good conversation offers an unspoken invitation for everyone to cocreate and discover something new. There is a kind of brilliance and luminosity to these larger conversations, and it is important that Co-Active Leaders in Front be able to generate conversations that are authentic, courageous, dynamic, and meaningful.

This can be difficult to do in our busy world, filled with terse e-mails and 140-character tweets. There's nothing wrong with these forums–they can be useful for communicating quick ideas or succinct information. But it's important that we also continue to foster our ability to sink into meaningful conversation.

A really good conversation takes time and commitment. People need to remain curious and continue to explore the outermost edges of the subject. Any meaningful conversation also requires courage because it calls us to question our most cherished beliefs and to be willing to explore the unknown.

In an article for the Leader to Leader Institute, poet David Whyte says, "The best conversations make clear distinctions between what has gone before and what is now possible. They give the sense that we are part of something that is enlarging us or our organization rather than confining us. . . . You can get a hint of what these courageous conversations are by asking yourself, "What is the courageous conversation that I'm *not* having right now?"[3]

By looking for what is *not* being explored or spoken, Co-Active Leaders in Front will find the raw materials for courageous conversations that move a group beyond being defined by past successes and into a new and fresh territory.

Here is an example of how one Co-Active Leader in Front gave everyone in her division an opportunity to "weigh in and buy in" by leading a courageous conversation.

One of our Co-Active coaches was working with the retail division of a large marketing services corporation. Once the highest-performing division in the organization, the division had begun to slide. It was missing its targets, and engagement was at an all-time low. A new division president was hired to turn things around.

The new president decided to begin by initiating a courageous conversation with her executive team. "I'm the new kid on the block, and I really need your help," she said. She then asked the team, "What has been missing in the leadership of this division that has resulted in such poor performance? Why is engagement so low?"

There was an uncomfortable pause, and several people cleared their throats. For a time, there was superficial talk, blaming this, pointing to that. It wasn't going anywhere. Finally the new president held up her hand to stop the conversation. "This conversation isn't really telling us anything new. It sounds like the same old story that I've heard since the day I got here. The market is slow. Our competitors are gaining ground. The former president was a pain. . . . I already *know* all this.

"I want to have a different kind of conversation, a courageous one where we really lean into each other," she said. "When I asked what has been missing in the leadership of this division, I was talking about *your* leadership. When I asked you why engagement is so low, I was talking about *your* engagement." She continued calmly, "We need to change things in this division or we might not survive. We certainly won't *thrive*. I can't do that by myself. I really do need your help." Then she repeated her initial questions.

One at a time, the team members began to speak more authentically. One said that the former president had run things so tightly that over time, innovation and creativity had withered. Another admitted that eventually he had given up and had started "phoning it in" a bit. Another nodded, saying, "I'm ashamed to admit it–that's true for me, too." Several other team members raised their hands in agreement.

Slowly, as the courageous conversation continued, others spoke to how things had slipped over time, with accountability and performance metrics slowly disintegrating and people (including themselves) caring less and less about top performance.

Though the conversation took time and was somewhat difficult, it cleared the way for what was to come. After each team member had had a chance to speak to the problem, the president asked team members why they had come to work for the organization in the first place and what they needed to be re-energized and inspired, once again, to do their very best. As people shared even more personally, they started getting inspired.

The president then outlined her vision for what was possible moving forward. "What do you think? What would you change? Where are the holes?" There was more courageous conversation as team members weighed in on where they were going and what would be needed to get there.

Finally the president paused and took a deep breath. "This success will not be possible without all of us working together," she said. "And while I understand how it happened, this kind of complacency won't get us where we need to go. Moving forward, I believe it will be unacceptable. What do you think?"

In the pause that followed, an older team member tapped his hand on the table firmly. "Unacceptable," he said. "Unacceptable," said another. Each executive followed suit, declaring his or her commitment to work together to raise the bar. Together they got down to it. They started holding each other accountable and asking hard questions when performance was substandard.

Not everyone on the team was able to make the shift. Old habits die hard, and eventually one of the team members decided to leave. Although this was difficult for everyone, the team remained committed to holding the highest standards. As the president continued to foster honest, transparent, and courageous conversations, she won her team's respect and trust. The culture and the division's performance shifted dramatically.

What would be different in our world if our Leaders in Front were able to engage and inspire their people through this kind of dynamic and courageous conversation?

Transparency is another way that Co-Active Leaders in Front generate connection and engagement. Transparency is so rare these days that it has a breathtaking impact when it does occur. Nothing generates trust more than when Leaders in Front tell the truth and speak openly. People know when the truth is being spoken. They do not have to be told.

If there is failure, then it is important to say cleanly, "I made a mistake, and here's how I'm going to take responsibility for it." This kind of honesty is vital to creating an atmosphere of safety, openness, and freedom to fail and learn.

We are not talking about needing to trot out loads of personal matters. What we are referring to here is simple honesty and authenticity. We've all been trained from an early age to keep it together—to look good and get it right. A bit of messiness and humanity is a welcome relief to most, and when Co-Active Leaders in Front are real, everyone else can relax a bit as well.

While this lack of transparency permeates our professional environment, it also colors our personal lives. A married couple is having difficulty, and it is becoming clear that they are not going to make it. However, they want to keep it together "for the kids." A big lie starts to fester, with everyone colluding to preserve the illusion that everything is just fine.

This absence of transparency does not serve anyone, most of all children. Young people have an uncanny knack for knowing the real score, and it's important for parents to treat their children with respect and let them know the truth of what is happening.

Karen remembers being eleven when her grandfather was dying of cancer. No one would say he was dying; rather, they would say that he was "tired and needed to rest." The intent of this misrepresentation was to protect Karen, but instead it was extremely frightening and confusing.

Sometimes people will use the *appearance* of transparency to manipulate emotions. The problem is, nobody really buys it. Transparency is not just the words that are said. It is about the energy and the authentic emotion with which the words are offered. People can usually sense the difference between the pretense of emotion and authentic emotion. When used as a manipulation, this pretense doesn't have the same resonance and instead feels like bad acting.

Politicians are famous for using the appearance of transparency to manipulate our emotions, as is the media. This kind of manipulation diminishes trust and confidence because it is not authentic and real. Whether or not they can articulate it, people can usually feel the difference and are consistently drawn toward Co-Active Leaders in Front who are transparent and real and who speak authentically from their heart.

What Is the *Active?*

The most important action of Co-Active Leader in Front is taking a stand for purpose and vision in the face of opposing forces in a way that is inspirational.

The epic trilogy *The Lord of the Rings*, by J. R. R. Tolkien, contains a shining example of what it means for a Leader in Front to truly take a stand. In both the book and the movie, Frodo and the other members of the Fellowship are making their way through the mines of Moria, with a demon Balrog in hot pursuit. The Balrog is gaining ground, and it's clear that Frodo and his companions will be overtaken. The quest will come to an end. The Fellowship will not make it out of the mines alive.

As a last measure, the wizard Gandalf takes a stand. He turns to face the approaching Balrog, which is about ten times his size, and, lifting his staff high into the air, spreads his arms wide and shouts, with all the conviction of his wizard's heart, "YOU! SHALL! NOT! PASS!"[4] The Balrog is vanquished. Frodo and the Fellowship are saved to continue on their quest, and Gandalf is ultimately transformed from Gandalf the Grey to Gandalf the White.

Just like the quest of the Fellowship, worthy endeavors are likely to involve opposition or challenge. As Co-Active Leaders in Front, when we are clear about what we stand for, we are able to move beyond ego, beyond being comfortable, looking good, and the external trappings of success. We stand firmly for our vision in a way that protects and nourishes everyone in the face of forces way beyond our control.

When we are clear and committed, we don't stand blindly or senselessly. Instead, we stand with all our senses fully open and our awareness stretching out to its farthest edges in the firm belief that the turbulence swirling around us is an integral part of our path of responsibility for our world. We stand in partnership with all the people we cherish, knowing that every challenge will only deepen our belief in our vision and solidify our certainty that we are creating that vision every day.

As with Gandalf in *The Lord of the Rings*, taking a stand in this way is deeply transformative because it illuminates one's power and vision in a larger way than is available in the day-to-day. Through ongoing challenge, we can reinvent ourselves repeatedly. As we are pushed to dig ever deeper, we are able to discover the ever-greater resonance and truth in our vision.

What About the Hyphen?

As we said in our opening chapter, the hyphen in Co-Active is important because it represents the "both and" rather than "either/or" of Co-Active Leadership. To thrive as a Co-Active Leader in Front, one must embrace paradox.

In general, people aren't comfortable with paradox and there can be a great deal of pressure on Leaders in Front to provide immediate and yet innovative solutions.

However, if there is no room for the unknown, it is unlikely that the answers and solutions will truly be innovative or will create much forward momentum. It is unreasonable to expect Co-Active Leaders in Front to nail the solution every time, right out of the gate. It is only when we teach ourselves to become comfortable with the unknown and to embrace paradox that we can truly evolve.

When we are required to immediately have the answer and get things right the first time, a certain rigidity ensues. We have to stay within what is known because we can't afford to fail. When we can see that everything is partly true and lean into the rightness and wisdom of all aspects of a paradox without needing to select the "right" one, then Co-Active Leader in Front comes alive.

Stepping into the unknown takes great courage, which is also an expression of the "both and" of Co-Active Leader in Front. This is illustrated by our favorite definition of the word *courage*, which is "rage of the heart," from the French *coeur* ("heart") and *rage*, as in passion.

Norman Vincent Peale, author of *The Power of Positive Thinking*, has been famously quoted as saying, "Throw your heart over the fence, and the rest will follow."[5] Just like the rider of a horse approaching a challenging jump, Co-Active Leaders in Front must be present to the rage and passion in their hearts (*co*) and at the same time throw their hearts out in front of themselves past any obstacle and in front of the fear (*active*). Without this courage, this "rage of the heart," we will never be able to make those daring leaps into the unknown, where new discoveries await.

Co-Active Leaders in Front must make peace with both failure and success and be able to create action and forward momentum from either one. They must be willing to look like a fool, stumbling and recovering over and over again for the sake of their vision and the people who are following them.

Finally, Co-Active Leaders in Front need to be able to both step forward *and* sit down, moving fluidly to Co-Active Leader Behind and encouraging someone else to take the helm when needed. This is another expression of the "both and" that lies at the heart of Co-Active Leadership–the paradox of holding a fierce commitment to a vision and at the same time remaining open and receptive to letting go and allowing others to take the lead sometimes.

It's great to be able to be responsible for our world from another dimension rather than remaining trapped in Leader in Front just because it is our position or title. This agility brings life and range to our leadership and also provides lots of opportunities for Co-Active Leaders in Front to engage with their most important job, which is growing leadership in others.

The hard part is to make the choice to sit down by moving to Co-Active Leader Behind and champion someone else's leadership. This requires paying attention, letting go, and having an exquisite level of trust.

Many of our clients work in classical hierarchical companies, and it can be quite difficult to let someone else take the reins, particularly if the person at the front feels that he or she is supposed to be the one with the answers. However, we have repeatedly seen the positive impact when Co-Active Leaders in Front shift and, rather than trying to do it all alone, empower leadership in others.

One of our colleagues, Arnie, was the director of a national nonprofit organization. For some time he had been racking his brain trying to come up with a new idea for the organization's annual fundraiser.

One day, two of the youngest people on his staff stepped into Arnie's office and said they had something they wanted to show him if he was interested. The staffers then outlined an innovative and creative idea for a fundraiser using social media. Arnie didn't know all that much about social media, but he thought the youngsters were on to something, and after working with them a bit, he gave them a budget and told them to run with it, that he had their backs. Arnie had the wisdom and the agility to "sit down" and begin leading from behind.

The two young staff people took full responsibility for the fundraiser, working long hours to ensure that it was a success. Throughout, Arnie cheered from the sidelines, encouraging them to believe in themselves and to keep going for it. When the fundraiser was a huge success, Arnie made sure that his young team members got all the credit.

The gift of Co-Active Leadership is that it fosters a dynamic rather than static relationship between a leader and his or her world. Imagine the impact if our Leaders in Front became more facile with shifting to Leader Behind. This choice alone would generate a dramatic shift in our current leadership paradigm and encourage responsibility at every level in our organizations, our families, and our world.

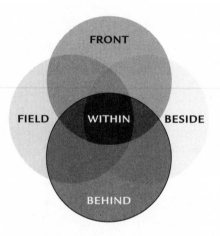

5

Co-Active Leader Behind

In the last chapter, we discussed how important it was for Leaders in Front to have the agility to sit down and allow others to step forward by moving to the dimension of Leader Behind. It's important to note that sitting down does not mean sitting back. Co-Active Leader Behind is not about sitting back, taking a break, abdicating, or being a passenger.

Co-Active Leader Behind is perhaps the most misunderstood of the dimensions. In command-and-control, one-dimensional leadership, we believe that "front" is better than "behind" because we believe that the Leaders in Front have all the power and influence. This creates a sense that everyone else is powerless and therefore should abdicate responsibility and follow blindly.

Make no mistake: Leaders Behind have the power to make or break any endeavor. When those behind are not willing to choose responsibility, it sucks the life out of any community or organization, generating separation and divisiveness. Blame and victimhood reign along with resentment, backbiting, and collusion.

Successful Co-Active Leaders Behind know they matter and understand the importance of their contribution, taking great pride in providing what is needed behind the scenes and out of the spotlight's glare. These Co-Active leaders are both the glue that holds everyone together (*co*) and the ones who provide the resources needed for things to go well (*active*). Co-Active Leaders Behind give themselves fully to the joy of participation and love, nourishing the brilliance in others because they know this adds to the goodness and the wholeness for all.

What Is Co-Active Leader Behind?

Co-Active Leader Behind is expressed through inclusive, dynamic followership.

The essence of Co-Active Leader Behind is service to others. Co-Active Leaders Behind trust the character and strength of the Co-Active Leader in Front and seek to evoke leadership in others by listening deeply, championing and acknowledging, and fostering wholeness through impeccability and integrity.

When Co-Active Leaders Behind give themselves wholeheartedly to serving the leadership and expression of others, they generate an inspirational sense of everyone working together. Co-Active Leaders Behind *know* they are responsible for their world. They don't need a title to tell them so.

There's a wonderful TED talk by Derek Sivers titled "How to Create a Movement."[6] Only three minutes long, the video clearly conveys the power and impact of Co-Active Leaders Behind. In the video, which was shot at an outdoor concert, one man (whom Sivers identifies as a "lone nut") stands up and begins dancing wildly. Then another person joins in, and Sivers makes the point that it is the *second* person, not the first, who grounds the action, taking it from the crazy and isolated movement of a "lone nut" to something worth following. As the video progresses, more and more people join in. Soon, everyone is dancing wildly and freely. The concert is transformed from an audience of observers to a community of wholehearted participants, actively cocreating a world of celebration.

This is the power of Co-Active Leader Behind. While the master creates the philosophy of any movement, it is the disciples who bring the work fully into existence and make it real and lasting. When they follow wholeheartedly and fully, Co-Active Leaders Behind have a tremendous impact.

Co-Active Leaders Behind also take responsibility for whom they are following and why. They do not follow blindly. Instead, they are willing to face the risks of challenging and asking questions to keep Leaders in Front in touch with and in tune with the vision. Instead of following halfheartedly and holding back vulnerability in case things don't work out, Co-Active Leaders Behind give 100 percent of themselves, offering whatever is needed to move the action forward for everyone.

Not every community or organization is ready to embrace multidimensional leadership, and those at the top are sometimes attached to position and power. Co-Active Leaders Behind need to remember that powerlessness is a two-way collusion; complying and "going along to get along" come at a very high price and only keep the power imbalance in place. If there is truly no willingness to value the input and contribution of Co-Active Leaders Behind, then it may be time for those leaders to find another environment that is more committed to collaboration and wholeness.

What Is the *Co*?

Mahatma Gandhi said, "The best way to find yourself is to lose yourself in the service of others." In the *co* of Co-Active Leader Behind, one's heart is filled with generosity and gratitude for being able to nurture the dream of the world through serving others.

Often, in one-dimensional leadership, we view serving as transactional rather than relational. Because we are scrambling to advance our position and climb the ladder to the top, our attention is focused on making sure that what comes back to us is of equal or greater value than what we gave. In this transactional framework, much of the shimmer and magic of service is lost because there is an expectation or a need waiting to be met. Real service creates intimacy and connection because it stems from a sense of abundance and generosity and a deep desire to contribute.

Some years ago, Henry, one of the authors of this book, was an assistant at a weeklong outdoor program that began with an eight-mile hike into an isolated wilderness area. The twenty participants were to live together for several days, working as a community to make camp, prepare meals, and do introspective work to prepare for the solo experience that was to come.

The solo was the highlight of the week, with each person in the group camping in isolation for several days and nights with water but no food. Participants returned from this experience at high noon on a very warm and sunny July day. Dusty and hot, they trudged back into the main camp after days of talking to no one. Rather than rushing up to greet everyone with lots of excitement and noise, Henry and his team welcomed people silently and led them to a shady spot, gently inviting them to sit down on a circle of waiting stumps and logs. There, the participants were provided with bowls of warm water to wash dirty hands and tired feet and were given plates of fresh fruit with which to break the fast. Henry and his colleagues went around the circle, kneeling in front of each person and offering these gifts simply and humbly. There was tremendous emotion on both sides, and it was clear that both the assistants and the participants were deeply nourished by this openhearted act of service.

While the love with which Henry and his team offered their gifts was a vital part of being Co-Active Leaders Behind, the thoughtfulness in anticipating what would most nourish and serve had quite an impact: cool shade on a hot day, warm water with which to soothe tired feet, ripe fruit to nourish the body. Service to others means that there is eagerness and joy in providing whatever is most needed, and thoughtfulness in anticipating it.

Anticipating what will most serve is a hallmark of great service. Recall your favorite visit to a restaurant or hotel. Perhaps the person at reception already knew your name. Perhaps you were welcomed with a warm towel or a cool drink after a long, hot drive from the airport. Or perhaps your waiter remembered you from your last visit and recalled your favorite cocktail or dish. Thoughtfulness and anticipation of the details causes people to feel valued whatever the setting, whether at a family gathering or in an organization.

Like Leaders in Front, Leaders Behind are looking ahead. However, instead of looking for *where* to go, they are looking for what might be needed *as* we go. By being fully present and anticipating what might be needed, Co-Active Leaders Behind can smooth out the potentially bumpy places on the journey, making it easier going for everyone.

This is not about the rigidity that comes with trying to be sure that there are never any bumps. Actually, a few bumpy places are needed and important. Surprises lend richness and offer learning on the journey. When Leaders Behind anticipate well, the bumps center on new discoveries and learning rather than struggling because insufficient thought and care was giving in planning.

In addition to serving others, finding others right orients Co-Active Leaders Behind toward looking for and appreciating value rather than being critical and always spotting problems.

Finding others right means we anticipate that others will likely make mistakes, and we are willing to have room for their humanness and fallibility. When we are willing to find others right, we are willing to forgive mistakes and blunders and can support others in taking responsibility for their mistakes in an encouraging rather than punishing way.

When we can find the rightness of a situation or a person, our perspective shifts dramatically. The circumstances change from "unworkable" to "possible." This shift in perspective creates our world.

Have you ever noticed that once you start thinking about buying, for example, a blue Mini Cooper, all you see on the road are blue Minis? We see what we are looking for. If we are looking for problems and unworkability, that's what we will find. If we are looking for opportunity and possibility, we will create that also.

Imagine if we were to find others right *first*, knowing that people make mistakes and will need to make course corrections along the way. Instead of looking for flaws and doing our best to cut others down to size, what if we started by looking for the value and usefulness in what was being offered? Imagine what would be possible if, rather than having to *watch* their backs, people had Co-Active Leaders Behind *at* their back, serving and supporting.

This doesn't mean that Leaders Behind just say yes and follow blindly. As we said earlier, Leaders Behind must be responsible for whom they choose to follow. If there is not wholeness and goodness at the front, then it is the responsibility of Leaders Behind to say so or to follow elsewhere.

Impeccability lays the foundation for the affirmative openheartedness of Co-Active Leader Behind. In *The Four Agreements*, by Don Miguel Ruiz, the first agreement is "Be Impeccable With Your Word." Here's how Ruiz describes this agreement: "Be Impeccable With Your Word. Speak with integrity. Say only what you mean. Avoid using the word to speak against yourself or to gossip about others. Use the power of your word in the direction of truth and love."[7]

Our words have huge power to create our world. Sometimes we don't realize that what we say and who we are being as we say it have everything to do with how things go in our lives.

Gossip is a cancer that can eat away at any community, be it an organization or a family. Gossip happens behind the scenes in the dark, so it is both toxic and elusive. Because issues are not dealt with in a forthright way, rumors spread. It becomes very difficult to know what is really going on and therefore what to trust.

Impeccability is a commitment to cleanliness in our communication. It ensures that conversations are courageous ones that foster wholeness and intimacy. Rather than gossiping around the water cooler, it's important to speak up and ask the question that is on everyone's mind.

This takes a great deal of courage. Regardless of how safe or secure the environment, it can still be frightening to be the one who says the emperor has no clothes. It's crucial that Co-Active Leaders Behind support each other in the courageousness of impeccability and that, in service to wholeness, they look for what else needs to be spoken rather than hanging each other out to dry.

What Is the *Active*?

The two most important *actions* of Leader Behind are believing and coaching.

If we are to truly serve others, we must be willing to actively express our belief in them. The coaching skills of acknowledgment and championing are two great ways to do this.

Acknowledgment is not the same thing as praise, nor is it simply a compliment. Praise focuses on appreciating what someone does. It's nice to receive praise for a job well done. Acknowledgment, however, can be transformative because it expresses belief in the character and inner strength of another. This supports people in recognizing gifts that they may have overlooked or dismissed, and it generates intimacy and connection because it strikes right at the heart of where someone is growing and getting stronger.

Heartfelt and authentic acknowledgment has the power to transform people and situations. Recently, two of our team members were attending a planning meeting at a very conservative client organization. The meeting was aimed at designing a one-day program to develop new competencies and teach people the Co-Active skills needed to step into a new role. Of the three people representing the client organization, Michelle was the only one familiar with the Co-Active model. As director of human resources, she had worked diligently for some time to introduce this relationship-based way of working to her organization. The other two representatives just weren't getting it. The group had been working together for an hour or more without much progress.

Acknowledgment came up as a potential content piece, and our team members began trying to capture, in words, the power and impact of acknowledgment. This is a bit like trying to describe a sunset to someone over the telephone. The visceral experience loses something in the translation.

All of a sudden, one of our team members turned to Michelle and blushed a little. Then she took a deep breath and looked Michelle squarely in the eye. "Michelle," she said, "you are a real pioneer. You've been working hard for a long time, risking it all to bring this important work to your organization. The people in your company will benefit tremendously from your willingness to be a Leader in Front and stand for what you believe is important."

The room became very quiet. Michelle began to tear up a little as the acknowledgment landed. No one needed to say anything. The impact of the acknowledgment was clearly felt, not just by Michelle, but also by everyone else in the room. After a moment or two, the group proceeded with their planning meeting, which moved forward with much more connection, heart, and engagement.

We get shy about acknowledgment. It's intimate to see another person deeply, and we tend to steer away from intimacy, even though it's something that we long for with all our hearts. It takes courage to risk, to be the first one to reach out and expose ourselves. There is such a need to look good and be cool and have our act together. There is such a fear of being seen as corny or goofy or weak.

Yet, being authentically seen by others is like water and sunshine for a plant–it expands us. Acknowledgment connects Co-Active Leaders Behind to a place of humanity and heart so that they can grow the best in others.

Championing someone is an absolute act of belief. When we champion, we plant the other person's flag on the hill that lies ahead and let him or her know that we are on the sidelines cheering wildly and believing fully in our hearts that he or she will prevail.

Championing another person is a powerful way to encourage risk taking and expansion. On the way to meaningful success, there will inevitably be failure and course correction. It's easy to get discouraged and give up. When we champion someone, our belief and faith inspires him or her to keep going past the challenging parts and on to eventual success. To continually reach for the extraordinary, we need to know that we have people championing us as Co-Active Leaders Behind.

Several years ago, Karen's youngest sister, Martha, encouraged her to give running a go and challenged her to run the San Francisco Half Marathon. Though filled with a longing to feel the wind in her hair, Karen was fairly doubtful. She was fifty-seven at the time and pretty sure that she was too old to take up running. Martha was certain that Karen could succeed.

When Karen started training, she was able to run only sporadically with lots of walking in between. Still, Martha remained convinced that Karen could become a runner. She checked in frequently and celebrated the smallest successes. She declared that she would run alongside her older sister. Eventually, Martha's confidence in Karen prevailed. Karen's speed and distance slowly increased.

The day of the race arrived, and Karen felt both prepared and nervous. The weather was awful–cold and foggy with a brisk headwind. However, excitement and adrenaline were flowing freely at the start, and the two sisters set off running together in the early-morning dark.

Though fully capable of a faster speed, Martha stayed with Karen every step of the way. When Karen was ready to pack it in halfway through, Martha refused to give up, letting her sister know in no uncertain terms that quitting at this point was complete nonsense and not the stuff of which Karen was made.

Together they crossed the finish line, running on pace and flying high. Though that was quite a victory, the deepening of their relationship and their love for each other was the biggest win. Yes, Karen worked hard and trained regularly. However, it was her sister Martha who championed her and kept her going through all the inevitable ups and downs on the way to success.

Co-Active Leaders Behind also use the coaching skills of deep listening and powerful questions to evoke the creativity and brilliance of others.

Listening deeply to another person has a tremendous impact. There's no better way to serve and nourish the magnificence in another person than to simply listen to him or her openheartedly and without judgment.

Unfortunately, listening deeply to another person has become rare. We are so focused on results and outcomes, and this fosters a preoccupation with the task rather than the people. In the pressure cooker of our daily lives, we are usually behind, running hard to catch up and make our way through our very long to-do lists. At work, we are under huge pressure to deliver results. We rush home and try hard to get everything done before we fall into bed exhausted. Even with our children, we often listen superficially because we are so preoccupied by the many tasks that fill our lives.

Also, we tend to listen to the words that are being spoken with a heavy emphasis on what is being said. Think of all the fights you have had centering on what was or was not being said. "That's what you *said*!" "Yes, but it's not what I *meant*!" "Well, it's what you *said*." Sound at all familiar?

For Co-Active Leaders Behind, it is important to listen beyond the words into the heart of the other person. We must be present enough and receptive enough to "hear" with our whole being beyond just the words that are being spoken.

This can be more challenging than it sounds. Our mind chatter can often be loud and demanding, nattering away about all kinds of opinions, judgments, and personal concerns. It takes practice and discipline to shift our attention beyond our internal dialogue and focus it firmly on another person.

It's helpful to imagine our listening as a spotlight. When we are listening to our own internal dialog, that's what gets illuminated. When we discipline ourselves to point the spotlight of our listening toward another person, the impact can be tremendous.

One of our clients offered us this beautiful story about the power of listening. George was a busy entrepreneur, and although he loved his children deeply, he was often preoccupied with his business and listened halfheartedly to their ramblings.

One evening, his six-year-old daughter was trying to talk with him about her cat, Puffy Gold, who had recently died and was buried in the backyard. Our busy entrepreneur was responding with the usual vague superficial listening sounds of "Hmm" and "Ahh." All of a sudden, his daughter climbed into his lap, placed one hand on either side of George's face, and turned his head firmly until he was facing her. Looking right into her father's eyes, she cried, "You are *not* listening to me, Daddy!"

Her father took a deep breath and set aside everything else but his daughter. Drawing her close, he asked her what she missed most about Puffy Gold now that the cat was gone. This was his daughter's first brush with death, and rather than trying to explain things or fix the problem, George asked her what she thought about death and what that meant to her. He asked her if her heart hurt and what that felt like. George slowed things way down and listened deeply to his daughter's responses.

Soon it was time for bed, and as George kissed his lovely daughter goodnight, he saw her clearly, not just as his child but also as a very special young person going through an important life transition. He'd been so busy and preoccupied that he'd almost missed it.

As this story illustrates, deep listening leads to curiosity, and expansive, open-ended questions naturally ensue. These questions are powerful because they encourage the other person to reflect on what lies within her and what is most meaningful and true for *her*, not for the listener. In this story, it was important for George's daughter to find her own way and to come to her own conclusions without someone else telling her what was important or true.

The very best and most valuable questions we can ask another are simple and innocent. What matters about that? What is most important to you here? What do you think, feel, and want? These questions let go of knowing and of providing information or a point of view and instead open up the internal knowing of another. Our interest in the other person's experience and the openheartedness and simplicity of our questions create enormous room for some-one to expand and grow.

We all have within us a number of creative responses to the challenges we face, and the answers we discover for ourselves are usually what hold the most resonance and meaning. Coaching provides a powerful context for this discovery.

What about the Hyphen?

The hyphen of Co-Active Leader Behind rests in knowing that one is *responsible* without being *in charge* and makes it clear that Co-Active leadership is not defined by one's position but by one's contribution and willingness to be responsible for one's world.

This expands the creativity and resourcefulness that are available to all and ensures that we are all sticking together and moving together while at the same time fostering ownership of what is unfolding.

Co-Active Leader Behind can be nourishing and fulfilling. When it is appreciated and valued, when it is practiced with sincerity, it lifts us out of any victim story we might have lingering and allows us to live and work together with our hearts at peace. We are able to rest in the joy of service and the inherent knowledge that we are creating our world together every day in a way that is important, connected, and real.

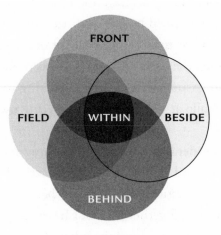

6

Co-Active Leader Beside

One-dimensional leadership models foster the myth that it is more expedient and efficient to have just one person in each position. Power must be held by one person only so that it is clear who has the power and authority and exactly whom we should blame when things go wrong.

Also, as we become ever more action oriented and results driven, it appears that there isn't time for all this relationship stuff. It's faster and more efficient to just do it ourselves without bothering too much with other people.

This imbalance between *active* and *co* permeates much of our lives, with relationships and interconnectedness getting sacrificed as we push ourselves to do more, produce more, accomplish more on our own. While in the short term it might feel as if we are effective, we are shortsightedly cutting ourselves off from the creativity and synergy that are available only through partnership with other people.

Isolation and separateness are actually an illusion. In truth, everything we do occurs in relationship with someone else. Whether that relationship is nourishing or debilitating is up to us. We are by nature communal creatures, designed to live and work in partnership with others. We are most effective when we are able to lean in fully to the resource of the other people in our lives. The dimension of Co-Active Leader Beside brings awareness and responsibility to these partnerships so that we can work together more effectively, creatively, and joyfully.

What Is Co-Active Leader Beside?

Most of the time, co-leading consists of dividing responsibilities and a "your turn, my turn" way of doing things. Co-Active Leader Beside is a true partnership, with both people being fully responsible for every part of the initiative. Co-Active Leaders Beside take responsibility for their world by creating their partnership around a shared vision and intention and supporting each other's strength to generate a powerful synergy in which the whole is much greater than the sum of the parts.

Co-Active Leader Beside is like a masterful dance with both parties leaning in 100 percent and each very sensitive to the direction of the other. In this dance, both leaders balance 100 percent commitment with complete humility, being willing to take the lead or follow in each moment. So, as with any great dance pair, it is impossible to tell who is leading and who is following because each one owns the whole thing at the same time.

Co-Active Leaders Beside often finish each other's sentences. They will enthusiastically disagree. If one is headed off in the wrong direction, the other will break in and redirect. Rather than creating *with* each other, Co-Active Leaders Beside create *from* each other. Because they are aligned around their vision and direction, they lead together in an improvisational way that is fresh, alive, and engaging.

When we choose the dimension of Co-Active Leader Beside, we are able to reach higher and risk more because we know that someone is holding our rope and we are holding his. If we fall, we won't fall flat on our face because our partner, our co-leader, will be there to catch us. We are more awake and more alive because we know that we need to be ready to catch our partner as well.

When someone is walking beside us, we have more courage to walk into the unknown and to risk the dark and messy places in our journey. Most of us knew this instinctively as children. We would bring a sibling or a friend with us when we knew we were in trouble with parents or authorities. We would take a dare from that same friend, testing our courage in a way that we would never dream of doing on our own. We were often more alive in those relationships than we were anywhere else. When did we grow up and begin to think it was somehow better to do things alone?

By way of supporting the best in each other, Co-Active Leaders Beside hold each other accountable for integrity and also for the vision and direction of where they are headed together. Many leaders these days are not held accountable by anyone, which results in all kinds of bad behavior. Ego-driven behavior and misuse of power become less likely when there are two Co-Active Leaders Beside.

When we first started working with a co-leader model in our programs at the Coaches Training Institute (CTI), we wanted to create an environment in which our students would move beyond aiming for the right answer and the right way. We discovered that with two co-leaders, students were much more likely to expand beyond one "right" answer and discover their own unique approach. What emerged was a kind of cellular learning in which our students were able to learn, evolve, and change at an essence level, far beyond simply memorizing content or trying to mimic the actions of a single, charismatic leader. Rather than adding more information to the file systems in their brains, people were able to incorporate material, fully own it, and then move beyond the data to generate and create their own individualized approach.

When two people step fully into Co-Active Leader Beside, they model a relationship that is human and authentic. This creates permission for others to do the same, fostering an environment of connection and aliveness rather than one of isolation and fear.

We also discovered that this dimension of Co-Active Leader Beside creates a deep sense of belonging for all, which is so important to our human nature. We all long to be seen, to be known, and to feel like we belong, and it is important to incorporate this sense of belonging into our workplaces and our communities, our countries, and our world. In the business and pace of our modern world, it is vital that we remain grounded and connected to one another and to the wholeness that we can generate together.

This sense of belonging is impossible to create if we need to keep looking good in order to maintain our position and power. In this situation, people feel isolated because they are forced to keep their authenticity hidden and reveal only the parts of themselves that are authorized as "professional" or appropriate. Co-Active Leaders Beside create safety for different expressions and different approaches, and others feel encouraged to be themselves and bring their own uniqueness and creativity to the matter at hand.

In Co-Active Leader Beside, it's important that both people remain grounded in Leader Within. Otherwise there is a risk of codependency or becoming so blended with the other person that we lose our sense of self and our own authentic voice. It is important to stay grounded in one's self-authority in Co-Active Leader Beside and to balance openness and a willingness with the understanding that there needs to be a flow of contributions from both sides. If you notice that you are giving more than 100 percent in Leader Beside, it's useful to step back a bit without blame and allow more room for the other person to contribute.

What Is the *Co*?

The *co* of Co-Active Leader Beside is intentionally designing our partnership with the person who is right beside us and leaning into that partnership 100 percent.

We use the term *designed alliance* to describe the *co* of Co-Active Leader Beside because it is an indication that the two partners are working side by side in service of a shared vision and outcome. Designing the alliance allows Co-Active Leaders Beside to get grounded in who they want to be and where they want to go together.

Designing an alliance begins by finding alignment around a common vision and direction; the next step focuses on establishing clear agreements about what each person will offer and bring to the partnership.

As the partnership unfolds over time, it is important to continue designing the alliance with both people taking full responsibility for keeping the relationship clear and bright. With designed alliance, any challenges and breakdowns in the relationship become an opportunity to redesign. This results in the relationship growing stronger, more intimate, and more alive over time.

In our work in organizations, we often give executives homework to design the alliance with their direct reports. While this is useful, most have found that designed alliance had the biggest impact in their relationships with their loved ones, most particularly their children.

It was incredibly moving to hear these high-powered executives talk about an intimate and transformative conversation they had with their child about an area that had previously been fractious and entrenched. With designed alliance, they were able to get on the same side of the issue with their child and stand side by side to generate a common resolution. This caused the child to feel seen, heard, and valued rather than corrected and judged, so the connection and sense of belonging opened up between parent and child.

One executive reported that her son was not doing well in school, even though he was quite bright. No matter how much she nagged or scolded him, her son resisted putting in the work needed to get good grades.

That evening, our executive tried a different approach. Instead of nagging, she sat down and talked with her son about what was most important to him about school and getting good grades. He said that he felt bored in school because it was not competitive enough. He indicated that he didn't care much about grades at that point in his life but might get interested in studying if it could be a game of sorts. He also let his mom know that he was so irritated by her constant nagging that he had started tuning her out.

They agreed to create a contract with a specific time frame. The son agreed to study regularly. His mother agreed that she would trust him and refrain from nagging. If the son accomplished a grade average of B or better, he would receive a prize. If he achieved straight As, the prize would be bigger. Both were excited about this new approach. Over the ensuing months, they joked and teased about this contract and whether one or the other of them might be moving toward violating the terms.

When the son achieved straight As, both were delighted and maybe a little surprised. The son got to pick out a new snowboard that he had been wanting, and his mother took him out for a grown-up dinner to celebrate. What mattered most to both of them, however, was the deepening of their relationship and the sense of being on the same side and working together.

To truly lead beside, we must be present with the person who is here in this particular moment as opposed to the person we wish were here or we think should be here.

It is easy to fall into the stories we make up about another person and completely miss the person who is right in front of us. We become angry and frustrated because the other person is not fitting into our picture, and we blame her for not acting as we think she should. We plan out the dialog we want to have and are disappointed when the other person does not know her lines.

In Co-Active Leader Beside, we must approach each moment with deep curiosity and openness. The past is gone forever, and the future is yet to come. All we really have is the present moment.

This curiosity and openness allow us to move past our judgments and assumptions and get into relationship with the person who is here now. Only then can we really connect and create from each other fully.

In the ten-month leadership program that we co-lead, there are many adventure-based physical challenges. One involves two people climbing up to two wires about thirty feet in the air. The wires extend from the central pole in the shape of a V, becoming wider apart the farther they get from the central pole. The goal is to move out on the wires together, leaning in to each other for support. It is essential that both partners be fully present with the person who is across from them *right now*. Any story that either has made up about who they need to be in relationship or whether their partner is up to the task will create immediate instability, and the pair will become wobbly and ungrounded.

As the partners venture farther out, they discover that the more they trust and lean in, the stronger and more solid both become. It is quite beautiful to see two people up there on the wires, leaning in and giving 100 percent to their partner and demanding the same in return. It's a profound metaphor for the full commitment of Co-Active Leader Beside and of both partners leaning in and calling each other forth 100 percent–100 percent through both the elegant and clumsy times.

Just like our participants up on the high wires, we may pull back when we feel frightened or unsure. Everything changes when we learn to counteract that urge to pull back and instead lean in 100 percent.

Often we *believe* that we are fully committed to another, and yet a part of us is holding back, keeping something in reserve in case things don't work out. That way, we can be sure that we can cover our own butt by hanging any failures on the other person. Sadly, this behavior is not all that unusual, as Martin's story attests.

Martin's manager assigned him to co-lead an important project with his co-worker Gary. Martin was excited about the project, which would put him in line for a big promotion if it was successful. He was not all that excited about working with Gary, as he had had several challenging altercations with Gary in the past. However, Martin really wanted to be seen as a team player, so he declared to anyone who would listen that he was going to give working with Gary a go, even though he knew it would be quite difficult.

As work on the project progressed, there was an underlying tension between the two men that never broke out in actual disagreement. Martin would frequently acquiesce to Gary's point of view. Gary would try to figure out what Martin really wanted.

When they were asked to make a presentation to the executive board, Martin was elated. This was his big chance to get ahead. During the presentation, Martin began to undermine Gary very subtly. While never disagreeing with anything Gary said, Martin tried hard to give the impression that he was the brains behind the project and that the project had moved forward successfully in spite of, not because of, his co-worker.

After Martin and Gary finished the presentation, the board members politely thanked them. Martin was promoted to a managerial position, where he continued to try to look good to his superiors by blaming any failures on someone else. He was not a popular manager and could not understand why his direct reports were so unappreciative of his efforts.

Martin's story is all too familiar. Particularly in the workplace, we have learned that we can get ahead only by pushing ourselves in front of someone else. We've also learned to avoid any kind of conflict or disagreement because it forces us to face the anger and hostility just beneath the surface. Unfortunately, these practices keep us stuck in the same place, recycling the same solutions. It is only through surfacing conflict in a clean way that we can move forward into new territory.

When there is friction and disagreement, 100 percent–100 percent means that both partners will stay with the conflict because they know that on the other side of the disagreement they will find a greater clarity and a more synergistic truth that is more profound and material to their shared vision.

Larger than the sum of the parts and far beyond a "win-win" compromise, this third way emerges from the creative combustion of two people engaging in both passionate discourse *and* deep listening long enough for a brand-new possibility to emerge . . . an option that was simply not accessible from inside each individual's point of view.

What Is the *Active*?

The *active* of Co-Active Leader Beside is about embracing disagreement for the sake of synergy.

As we said earlier in this chapter, the relationship between Co-Active Leaders Beside is something like a dance, with both people clear about direction and outcomes while at the same time giving themselves fully to the mystery of each moment. For this dance to be spontaneous, both people need to be aligned on a larger context, which is not the same thing as being in complete agreement about all the pieces.

Most of us approach another person as a collection of ideas, values, and beliefs with which we do or do not agree. We focus on the *what*, on the specific idea or solution. When another person is speaking, we are often listening from our own point of view and noticing whether we agree with what he is saying. The structure looks a bit like this:

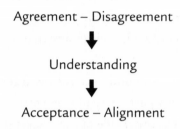

When we get together and start sharing ideas, eventually differences emerge, at which point we tend to dig in our heels and get very right. We debate. We get righteously committed to our point of view and lose our ability to be in relationship. Often we don't even see the other person as a fellow human being.

Sometimes we debate the issue long enough to find a compromise or a tolerated agreement. Sometimes we actually change the other person's point of view and she winds up agreeing with us. We then feel that we understand the other person and can accept her.

This approach doesn't deepen the intimacy of the relationship or increase each person's ability to create with and from each other in the moment. In seeking agreement as the first step in connection, we cut ourselves off from much of the creativity that is available.

This approach also limits the range of our interactions, as it tends to steer us toward people who mostly agree with our opinions and points of view–people who are most like us.

What if we were able to reverse the order of the process and begin with the *why* rather than the *what*? What if it looked like this?

Alignment – Acceptance

Understanding

Agreement – Disagreement

With designed alliance, Co-Active Leaders Beside have begun by aligning around a larger context and finding the commonality of purpose and vision. This creates a container for the partnership that is larger than any disagreement or conflict.

Once two Leaders Beside have found the larger alignment of purpose and vision, they fully understand or *stand under* the other's point of view without feeling threatened or having to decide which one is right and which one is wrong.

When there is alignment and understanding, it is much easier to navigate forward together, moving in and out of agreement. In fact, disagreements between the two Leaders Beside can become creative catalysts to finding new ways of resolving old problems.

Seeking alignment is a fairly unusual concept. Usually, we focus on the specific issue in an either/or way. Should we move to the country or continue living in the city? Should we send our child to public school or should we homeschool? Should we have national health care or not?

When we seek alignment around the larger context, we can find a place to stand together, even as we disagree about the particular issue. Why are we thinking about moving? What is most important about how we educate our child? What do we believe about the relationship between a government and its citizens? We can continue to disagree, all the while knowing that we are working from a similar context and are therefore united. Once there is alignment, it is much easier for people to empower forward action because there is a foundation of mutual respect and alignment on which to stand.

Another concept that fuels the dance of Co-Active Leaders Beside is the phrase "Yes, and . . ." This phrase is borrowed from the world of improvisation and is what allows improvisers to create, in the moment and on the spot, from whatever is handed to them. In an improvisation, it wouldn't work very well to say, "No, this is the wrong thing to be giving me right now" when handed an object. If your partner hands you a rubber chicken, your job is to be inspired by the rubber chicken and have the rubber chicken take you to places where you never would have been able to go without it. This is what makes improvisation so magical and alive.

In Co-Active Leader Beside, "Yes, and . . ." enhances the dance between the partners and supports their ability to create from and with each other in the moment.

The yes indicates appreciation as opposed to agreement and provides a fresh perspective from which to view another's contribution. Instead of looking for the problem or the area of disagreement with what the other person is saying, we are instead pointed toward finding value. This is not about complying or compromising in order to say yes to the whole thing. Instead, the yes is about looking into what is being offered and finding something to appreciate.

Next comes the *and* step, in which the partner adds his or her own contribution to whatever is being offered. It's important that this *and* is not a disguised *but*, which negates the initial offering or puts forward one's own version of a better idea. Instead, it is about appreciating the other person's contribution and then adding something of one's own to the creative build. This can go back and forth quite effortlessly as Co-Active Leaders Beside move forward together.

Here is an example:

LEADER ONE: "I think it would be a good idea to generate a weekly team meeting so that we can all stay on the same page and move in the same direction."

LEADER TWO: "Yes, it's important to get together, *and* I think meetings are a waste of time *and* the team won't really be interested. (Usually in examples like this, the and is said rather loudly and with extra emphasis.)

Can you see how Leader Two didn't appreciate Leader One's contribution? Actually, Leader Two was focused on spotting the problem with Leader One's idea and explaining why it would not work. With a simple shift, which is mostly energetic and not really in the words, the conversation could go like this:

LEADER ONE: "I think it would be a good idea to generate a weekly team meeting so that we can all stay on the same page and move in the same direction."

LEADER TWO: "Yes, it's important to have a weekly team meeting, and I think we can work together to create a structure that would be engaging and useful."

This might seem simplistic and maybe even a little corny. Try it for a day. Try going through just one day appreciating and finding value in whatever is being offered to you. Notice how this creates a different relationship with people in your life, one in which their contributions are valued and celebrated rather than immediately shot down. We all respond favorably to feeling valued and appreciated, and this approach opens up creativity and relationship.

People tend to avoid disagreement like the plague, primarily because they are afraid that disagreement will put the relationship at risk. Over time, those unexplored and unexpressed disagreements fester and become personal. Resentment and toleration thrive, and authenticity and trust go out the window.

Designed alliance, 100 percent–100 percent, and other tools of Co-Active Leader Beside create a context of trust and safety in which we are able to disagree with the idea or concept while still holding the other person with respect and regard.

What about the Hyphen?

As Co-Active Leaders Beside, two people stand as strong, grounded individuals while at the same time becoming one leader, moving in tandem with each other and united in a cocreated vision and direction. Co-Active Leaders Beside are two individual leaders and one leader at the same time. This paradox of Co-Active Leader Beside allows both parties to operate with full ownership, deep respect, and robust disagreement.

There is no one of us (or even a group of us) that has the whole answer to the challenges we face. No matter how insightful or brilliant we are, individually we can offer just a piece of the whole. It is only through dialogue, deep listening, and passionate disagreement that we find our way to something larger than a singular and isolated point of view. The more we are able to engage in enthusiastic disagreement with each other, the more we will be able to uncover the best in ourselves and each other.

In the Co-Active dance of Leader Beside, a synergy occurs. The overall impact is greater than the sum of the parts, and the impact of two Co-Active Leaders Beside is much greater than the total of their individual contributions. They step forward together in this synergy of relationship, taking responsibility for their world and cocreating that world together every day with every step. This synergistic power that is ignited by Co-Active Leader Beside is not only effective and energizing for the leaders but also dynamic and alive for others, and it creates a profound sense of belonging to something greater than any one leader could generate on his or her own.

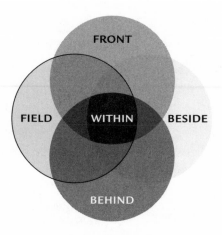

7

Co-Active Leader in the Field

There is an energetic field that surrounds all of life and is offering us information all the time. We might say that the field is "speaking" to us, even though there are no words.

One of our clients, Eric, recently told us this story about his experience with the energetic field. Eric, the chief information officer of a major training company, was changing planes in Indianapolis, Indiana. His first flight had been delayed, and he knew that he had to move fast in order to make his connection. So Eric was very irritated when he noticed that the concourse ahead of him was completely blocked with people. "How am I going to push my way through this mess?" he wondered.

As Eric drew closer, a wave of energy hit him that was both fierce and reverent. His heart skipped a beat, and he felt his irritation vanish. He could sense that something important was happening. Coming to a full stop, Eric looked out the window to his left and saw caskets being unloaded from a nearby jet and placed on a waiting truck. As each casket was unloaded, it was covered with a flag. There was silence. No one was moving.

Eric's eyes filled with tears, and he noticed tears in the eyes of others. He saw that many nationalities were represented in the group and that many had their hands over their hearts. As people approached from behind, they fell silent, swept up in the energy and intensity of the moment even before they could see what was happening. No one spoke a word, and yet everyone understood completely. Once the last casket was loaded onto the truck, people began silently moving again, making their way to their destinations.

We have all had experiences like this—times when we could sense and feel what was going on without needing to be told. We enter a party with a group of people, ready to have a good time, but as soon as we open the door, we can sense that something difficult has occurred. Or we approach a group of people and have the uncomfortable feeling that they have been talking about us.

These experiences are a natural part of being a sensing human being. They are not unusual or particularly strange. This is what we mean by the energetic field.

What Is Co-Active Leader in the Field?

Co-Active Leader in the Field is not about leading a project, a team, or even an organization. Instead, Co-Active Leader in the Field is about expanding our attention beyond individual people to connect with the energetic field that surrounds life. This energetic field is a place of imagination, instinct, intuition, and a deeper resonance and knowing than is available from what is already known or proved.

Our one-dimensional view of leadership generally consists of actions that are pragmatic and reasonable with plenty of evidentiary proof. Even when we sense that something is important, if it is not visible and provable, our world tends to treat it as if it doesn't really exist. As Co-Active Leaders in the Field, we refuse to accept that the only thing that exists is the factual, pragmatic reality that is right in front of us.

In order to create new ideas that are truly innovative, we must reach into the invisible and unseen with our imagination. As Antoine de Saint-Exupéry wrote in the French novella *The Little Prince*, "What is essential is invisible to the eye."[8]

As Co-Active Leaders in the Field, we notice and take responsibility for our impact in and on our world. If, as we said in chapter 1, leaders are those who are responsible for their world, the dimension of Co-Active Leader in the Field connects us to a global sense of the world we are creating.

As Co-Active Leaders in the Field, we have ownership of the whole of life on our planet. We understand that everything we do has an impact and reach for actions that serve rather than destroy life. We seek to create a world that works for everyone because as Co-Active Leaders in the Field, we understand that we are a part of everything that is happening in our larger world. We do, in fact, create our world together, every day, and all of our actions have an impact.

As life becomes more diverse and more complex, it will be vital to access the instinct, intuition, and innovation available in Co-Active Leader in the Field. While it is important to be aware of our past, we will not be able to resolve the challenges that face us from what is already known. To quote Albert Einstein, "We can't solve problems by using the same kind of thinking we used when we created them."

In the dimension of Co-Active Leader in the Field, we expand our sensory awareness so that we can access our imagination, intuition, and insight (*co*) and have the courage and commitment to act on what we sense in a way that is innovative and new (*active*).

The world of sports is filled with examples of Co-Active Leader in the Field. Wayne Gretzky, former Canadian ice hockey player and head coach, is famously quoted as saying, "I skate to where the puck is going to be, not where the puck has been."

How did Gretzky know where the puck was going to be? While training and experience certainly played a part, in the moment he wouldn't have had time to analyze reams of analytical data. Gretzky had to use his intuition and instinct (*co*) and then act on that instinct without stopping to check in with other people for their agreement (*active*).

High-tech innovation offers another example. Apple cofounder and CEO Steve Jobs was well known for going to a special room filled with physical prototypes of all the new products Apple was creating. Jobs and his lead designer, Jony Ive, would spend time together touching the various prototypes and sensing and feeling into what they believed would be most elegant and useful for Apple's customers. Perhaps this commitment to Co-Active Leader in the Field was a source of Jobs's uncanny ability to skate to where the puck was going to be by designing products that customers did not even know they wanted.

What Is the *Co?*

The *co* of Co-Active Leader in the Field requires that we let go of our need to find an immediate solution and slow down enough to access our intuition and insight. Once we let go of our need to find the one "right" answer and settle into the moment, our intuition will come forward and offer us insight that we are not able to access when we are hyperfocused on solving the problem in front of us.

This can be difficult in a world where we are trained to provide concrete answers and solutions that are based on proven practices. However, it is only by trusting enough to let go of what we know that we will be able to access our imagination, intuition, and insight.

The dictionary defines *intuition* as "our natural ability to know something without any proof or evidence" and *instinct* as "a way of behaving, thinking, or feeling that is not learned: a natural desire or tendency."

The commonality in both of these definitions is *natural*. We are born with intuition and instinct. Along the way, we can lose our connection with both of these things as we are trained that there is only one dimension, one answer, and one right way. We become so filled with all our knowledge that there isn't room for anything else.

In a high-wire trapeze act, there is a moment when the aerialist who is flying must let go completely in order to be caught. To be "caught" by new insight from the energetic field, we also must let go of what we know and be willing to trust our instinct and intuition beyond what we can explain. It is only when we soften our focus and sink into the present moment that we can begin to sense the patterns, cycles, and flow of energy that are moving around and through us.

Our imagination can assist us in accessing our intuition and insight. We often invite people to take an imaginary mini-helicopter ride above the current situation. From this expanded meta-view, they notice patterns and cycles that they could not see when they were in the thick of the situation. Their instinct and intuition kick in, and they often have flashes of insight that were not accessible when they were too close to the circumstances.

The *co* of Co-Active Leader in the Field is also about noticing our impact. Think of a pebble falling into pond. There is an initial impact as the pebble hits the water, but what follows is a much larger impact as ripples issue out from the pebble, sometimes even lapping against the shore.

Like the pebble in the example above, all too often we only notice our own experience of hitting the water and sinking to the bottom. Expanding our awareness to include the energetic field allows us to observe the whole of our impact beyond our own individual experience. We can sense the ripples, the water lapping at the shore, and the energetic resonance of the whole.

Think of a high school teacher droning on and on without noticing if the information is landing, or someone giving a dull

PowerPoint presentation featuring slides with reams of data in twelve-point type. Think of a recent flight where a passenger was talking so loudly on his cell phone that it was difficult for those around him to think. These are all examples of people who were so numb to the energetic field that they were unable to notice the ripples of impact they were having.

What Is the *Active*?

The *active* of Co-Active Leader in the field is about taking actions based on the insight that our intuition offers us without the security of evidentiary proof or agreement from the external world.

Letting go of the security of what is commonly understood requires a big leap of faith and a willingness to fall. We must have faith that there is something valuable in what our instinct and our intuition offer us beyond what we can define or explain.

When we choose the dimension of Co-Active Leader in the Field, our actions are innovative and fresh because they are not bound by past information or evidence. We have no way of knowing how things will turn out because we are acting with immediacy using our instinct and intuition of the moment. This takes courage, but it also offers tremendous freedom to experiment, fail, and recover. The more we can embrace failure, the more we will be able to open to it and the more confident and resilient we will become.

As we act, we must also stay present to the *co* of Co-Active Leader in the Field and be aware of our impact. When we are aware of our impact, we can notice whether our actions are working and, if needed, try something different.

It is important to remain unattached to having the "right" impact out of the gate. If we attempt to over-engineer our actions ahead of time so that we are sure we will never have an impact that meets with disapproval, we will remain within the boundaries of what is safe and comfortable. We will never access the experimentation and failure that are an essential part of learning and growth. We need to let our instincts and our intuition fly and then notice how things are landing rather than planning out everything ahead of time so that we don't cause trouble. There will almost always be more aliveness if we allow ourselves to act spontaneously.

If we are present to and aware of our impact, we can create from whatever happens. Our actions as Co-Active Leaders in the Field will be innovative and offer something new because they come from the deeper *co* of our intuition and instinct.

Because we have no data to "prove" what we believe to be true, we must remain patient and creative, looking for an opening for forward movement without becoming stuck in solving immediate problems. It's easy to get trapped by our ego's need for approval and become insecure, defensive, or judgmental.

The pace of our life and work demands a focus on what is right in front of us–the problem, the fire. The people in our lives are not always eager for a larger solution even if it is a better one.

In *The 7 Habits of Highly Effective People*, author Stephen R. Covey tells a wonderful story about a team making its way through a jungle.

Envision a group of producers cutting their way through the jungle with machetes. They're the producers, the problem solvers. They're cutting through the undergrowth, clearing it out.

The managers are behind them, sharpening their machetes, writing policy and procedure manuals, holding muscle development programs, bringing in improved technologies, and setting up working schedules and compensation programs for machete wielders.

The leader is the one who climbs the tallest tree, surveys the entire situation, and yells, "Wrong jungle!" But how do the busy, efficient producers and managers often respond? "Shut up! We're making progress."[9]

People are so addicted to producing results and to getting things done in the short term that they lose sight of the big picture and don't want to slow down long enough to consider other possibilities. This results in their making the same mistakes over and over again while learning nothing.

To discover new solutions, Co-Active Leaders in the Field must be willing to be the ones to shout "Wrong jungle!" even though it might take others a while to slow down enough to listen.

Co-Active Leaders in the Field understand that there is a greater truth beyond the limited confines of our ego. They do not come forward with new information in order to look good and succeed, though success does come. Instead, Co-Active Leaders in the Field understand that they are part of a much larger whole and, with passion and humility, reach to contribute to their world in the most expansive way possible.

What about the Hyphen?

As Co-Active Leaders in the Field, we understand that while we are all unique expressions of life, we are also interconnected. Our differences need not divide us because even as we are unique and individual, we are also all one.

Life, by its very nature, embraces diversity and strives to expand, evolve, grow, and change. *Something* is always trying to happen, and tapping into the energetic field provides us with an expanded and current slant on what that something might be.

In Co-Active Leader in the Field, we are able to embrace the mystery of life, understanding that we matter and we have an important part to play in the unfolding story of our world, while at the same trusting that we are held by a consciousness that is much larger than we can imagine. Life is both eager to express itself through our particular lens and offering its wisdom and beauty to us in every moment if only we are willing to slow down and receive it.

8

The Dance of the Dimensions

Now that you understand each dimension more fully, which one feels the most comfortable and familiar to you? Which one feels the most challenging? Your responses to these questions offer a useful guide for your own leadership development. At the end of this chapter, you'll find a graph of the key *co* and *active* practices for each of the five dimensions. We encourage you to experiment! The dimensions with which you feel most at home represent an easily accessible way to express your Co-Active Leadership. Expanding your facility with all the dimensions will bring agility and range to your leadership.

We tend to think about what we do in terms of specific roles, such as teacher, manager, CEO, student, child, and parent, and define what is required of us by the expectations that come with the role. Co-Active Leadership is not a role. It is a way of being and acting, and we can choose it from any role and in any given situation.

We can choose any dimension depending on the needs of the moment and move fluidly from one dimension to another beyond the expectations of whatever role we occupy. This is one of the many things that make Co-Active Leadership such an adventure. Curiosity and the willingness to experiment, to fail and recover, to learn and grow, are hallmarks of Co-Active Leadership.

While the big events of our lives create the impetus for change, it is the moment-by- moment choices that mold and shape us. By choosing to experiment and try new things regularly, we develop confidence in our ability to fail and recover in a range of different situations. Failure is a natural part of learning and developing, and it teaches us to be resolute and steadfast in our endeavors. The more we choose to experiment with the dimensions of Co-Active Leadership that are unfamiliar, the more we fortify our own self-confidence and our certainty that we will be able to weather whatever life might send our way.

We are conditioned to think that we are somehow all alone and that everything depends on our ability to be good enough, smart enough, and wise enough. We feel that in order to lead effectively, we must have all the answers and solutions already worked out on our own. This false sense of isolation is insidious and pervasive.

The dimensions of Co-Active Leadership help us access the resources that are available all around us if we can only open our hearts to each other and to our world. We have vast resources at our fingertips. They are within us in the depth of our Co-Active Leader Within. These resources offer themselves through the people we connect with in Co-Active Leader in Front, Behind, and Beside. They reverberate throughout the huge field of information in Co-Active Leader in the Field. When we truly grasp and experience the vast resources that are available to us, a whole new world becomes possible.

The Dimensions in Action

Here are a few examples of how people are using Co-Active Leadership in a variety of everyday situations.

ISABEL

One of our leadership program graduates, Isabel is a dedicated second-grade schoolteacher. She uses the Co-Active Leadership Model as a tool to teach her students about collaboration and responsibility.

Isabel began by sharing the Co-Active Leadership Model with her class and letting them know that this was "what I learned at my school." She then told her students that they were already leaders and that they could believe in themselves. She said that they were already Co-Active Leaders Within.

Isabel went on to say that she believed in them 100 percent. Her job, she said, was to encourage the leader within each of them (Co-Active Leader Behind). What would be different in each of our lives if Isabel had been *our* second-grade teacher?

When one of her students, Shane, claimed responsibility for the class pet, a turtle named Pete, Isabel helped Shane see that as a Co-Active Leader in Front, he wasn't alone. While he had the final authority and responsibility for Pete, an important part of his job was to make sure that everyone was involved. With Isabel's support, Shane led a conversation with the class about Pete's care.

Rather than fighting over who got to feed Pete, the class decided to pair up (Co-Active Leader Beside) and take turns feeding Pete and cleaning out the box that was his home. Shane was to check in with the whole class every week to see how it was going.

Co-Active Leaders in the making, the class embraced the process wholeheartedly. When squabbles broke out, as they inevitably did, the students resolved them together because as one student claimed, "Pete is our responsibility and he needs us."

After a few weeks, Shane decided that it was time to step down. He turned over the Co-Active Leader in Front role to another student, Andrea, and did his best to be a good Co-Active Leader Behind.

BRITTA

One of our organizational clients is a dynamic example of the Co-Active Leadership Model in action. Britta, the president of her organization, is a terrific Co-Active Leader in Front, connecting people through courageous conversation and transparency and standing fiercely for the organization's vision and purpose. At the same time, she is a member of several teams in the organization that are led by others. She is an enthusiastic Co-Active Leader Behind on these teams, seeking to serve the team leader or leaders with her openhearted support and participation; and she listens deeply, asks powerful questions, and champions her leader or leaders.

The organization has embraced the notion of Co-Active Leader Beside, and it is common to find two co-leaders assuming shared and passionate responsibility for a project or initiative. While they are 100 percent committed to each other as Co-Active Leaders Beside, their alliance is dynamic, lasting as long as is needed for the success of the initiative. Then the Co-Active Leader Beside partnership is dissolved, and the people move on to other dimensions.

The company has developed a practice of pausing for a minute of silence in the middle of each meeting so that people have a chance to slow down and connect with Co-Active Leader in the Field. "What am I sensing?" they ask themselves. "What is trying to emerge?" They take another five minutes or so to discuss their insights, often finding easy solutions to agenda items in the process.

Initially, many people in the organization resisted Co-Active Leader in the Field because they found it uncomfortable. Now many report that it is their favorite dimension because they feel it helps them connect with the resonance of their organization's mission in the world. They also report that they are becoming more aware of their impact on others and on the world.

While the organization is thriving, things aren't perfect. Some people felt the need for a more structured working environment and left. Over time, however, the culture has settled into one of Co-Active Leadership. There are still any number of challenges and issues. What's different is that people face these challenges together, using the full resources of the organization's people rather than having everyone operating in isolation, locked in one-dimensional hierarchical roles.

EDUARD

The Co-Active Leadership Model can be useful in all kinds of different situations, both personal and professional. One of our clients, Eduard, shared with us how he used the Co-Active Leadership Model with his five siblings.

Eduard had been feeling wistful for some time about the connections between his brothers and sisters. Though they had once been close, the deaths of their parents had rent the fabric of the family, and over time the siblings had drifted apart.

As a Co-Active Leader Within, Eduard realized that family was very important to him. Eduard was the eldest of the five, and, tired of wishful thinking, he decided to act.

He began by choosing Co-Active Leader Beside and called his sister Martine, asking her to be his co-leader in creating more intimacy and connection among the siblings. It took some time and patience, but finally Eduard and Martine were able to arrange a weekend gathering of all the siblings in Martine's home.

Over the weekend, Martine and Eduard shared their longing for more closeness and connection, but as often happens, the siblings fell into old patterns. The conversation continued to circle around and around with many excuses. Eduard kept pointing that out and was met with familiar resistance and resentment. He started to feel resentful himself.

Eduard then remembered Co-Active Leader in the Field. He took a breath and softened his focus. As he did so, he sensed a heavy weight lifting from his shoulders. He realized that he was caught in an old pattern himself. As usual, he was trying to force things. It was time to stop being the eldest sibling and let things unfold instead of always controlling them! He sat back.

Moving to Co-Active Leader Behind, Eduard acknowledged his siblings and began listening deeply. Once in a while, he asked a powerful question. Slowly the energy in the room began to change.

The siblings began to talk more intimately, eventually realizing that their grief over the deaths of their parents had come between them. They saw that they had been trapped in an old pattern of blaming each other (particularly Eduard) without owning their responsibility. They all realized that they longed to sustain their sense of family, and Marco, the youngest, agreed to take responsibility for arranging the next family gathering.

MELANIE

The Co-Active Leadership Model is an effective tool in working with teams. One of our leadership graduates, Melanie, shared with us how she used the Co-Active Leadership Model in her work with her team members as they implemented a new payroll system. Melanie began with Co-Active Leader in Front, scheduling several team meetings in which she outlined the project and encouraged courageous conversations about the overall vision and feasibility. These meetings did not go well, however. Everyone on the team was competing for airtime, interrupting each other without listening to anything else. Half the team seemed determined to take control; the other half seemed apathetic and bored.

Melanie decided to try a different dimension. She moved to Co-Active Leader Beside, and, meeting with each of the team members individually, she introduced them to the Co-Active Leadership Model. Melanie then went on to design an alliance with each team member based on his or her part of the project. This was quite impactful.

Melanie asked various team members to practice Co-Active Leader Beside, with different partnerships leading the next series of team meetings. During the meetings, Melanie asked everyone to practice Co-Active Leader Behind, which she also modeled beautifully. These meetings were much more successful.

After the meetings, Melanie continued to lead her team as a Co-Active Leader in Front, keeping them motivated, connected, and in sync.

One of Melanie's team members, Pamela, had a reputation for being difficult. Usually what Pamela had to say was quite valid. It was Pamela's delivery that was the issue. Over the course of the project, Melanie worked with Pamela as a Co-Active Leader Behind, providing honest feedback along with coaching and acknowledgment. Over time, Pamela came to trust Melanie and was willing to risk trying different approaches because she knew that Melanie was right there behind her every step of the way. Melanie shared that watching Pamela's transformation was one of the highlights of the experience.

Parallel testing was essential, and as the project approached its deadline, Melanie moved to Co-Active Leader in the Field, noticing that the tension in the team was mounting. No one was willing to say anything because they had all been trained to get the job done no matter what. Melanie followed her instinct to speak about the tension to the team. "We're going to be just fine," she said, "as long as we continue working together." Melanie watched the panic in the group subside.

ZACK

Zack, one of our colleagues, told us how he used the Co-Active Leadership Model during a speech he gave at his company. Zack was a relatively new CEO and wanted to create a more dynamic and inclusive culture in his organization.

Carefully, he prepared a speech for his entire company outlining his strategy for the coming year. Just as he was about to swing into the heart of his speech, Zack sensed that the group was not completely engaged.

Looking out at the crowd, he noticed that a few people were getting up to get coffee and others were texting on their cell phones. He paused for a moment and connected with Co-Active Leader in the Field. "I'm not reaching them," he thought. In a flash of insight, he realized that he had fallen into the very pattern of one-dimensional leadership that he was trying to break apart. "I'm talking *at* people, not *with* them," he realized.

Right in the middle of his talk, he set aside his prepared remarks and invited one of his executives, Angelique, to come forward and be a Co-Active Leader Beside with him.

Angelique and Zack took a moment to design their alliance, and then together they began to co-lead a conversation with the group about what the new plan really meant. Everyone quickly became more engaged.

The discussion centered around how important it was to protect the feeling of camaraderie in the organization while at the same time moving in a new and exciting direction. Zack and Angelique were informal and relaxed. When Zack struggled to find the right words, Angelique finished his sentence. Sometimes they interrupted each other, adding important context to what was being said. Together, they generated a synergistic message that was both inspiring *and* intimate.

The people in the group began to ask questions and share input and ideas. The excitement in the room grew. As the meeting drew to a close, Zack and Angelique received enthusiastic applause.

Experimenting with the Model

These examples are just a few of the ways to use the Co-Active Leadership Model. If people are competing for the lead on a team, try teaching them about the model and rotate the different dimensional roles in the group. When people have a role to play, leadership becomes multidimensional and everyone stops competing for the top.

If there is lax accountability and missed deadlines, try choosing Co-Active Leader in Front and point toward the lack of integrity by fostering courageous conversations about what's been getting in the way. Then ask people to recommit.

If two people are arguing repeatedly, help them practice the alignment process in Co-Active Leader Beside so that they can disagree more effectively. Or if people are rebellious, give Co-Active Leader Behind a try. Once people feel truly heard, seen, and supported, behavioral problems tend to ease.

If things feel strange or you feel caught in the details, take a breath and slow down a little. Relax and open up to Co-Active Leader in the Field. You might discover an important insight hovering just on the edge of your awareness. In your practice with the model, keep experimenting and trying new things. Encourage others to do the same.

Our beloved partner, Laura Whitworth, used to say, "The answer to the question 'How?' is 'Yes!'"[10]

We are not suggesting that practicing Co-Active Leadership is a magic bullet or that things will always work out the way you wish.

There will still be challenges, and it can take time and patience to evoke lasting change. However, once you say "Yes!" to responsibility and choose any one of the five dimensions, your world will begin to shift.

The people in the examples above are ordinary people, working in ordinary situations that many of us face in our lives. No one told them that they should take responsibility beyond the narrow definition of their role or title. This choice is available to people in any situation if they are willing to move beyond being passengers and take responsibility and ownership for their lives and their world.

Practices for Co-Active Leadership

(a chart that shows the five dimensions with the content below)

CO-ACTIVE LEADER WITHIN

Practice living from the inside out rather than the outside in.

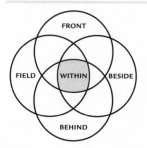

Co:
Nourish self-acceptance.
Let go of limiting beliefs.

Active:
Clarify your personal values.
Discover your life purpose.

CO-ACTIVE LEADER IN FRONT

Practice generating connection and inspiration.

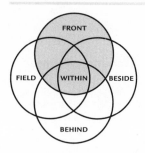

Co:
Encourage courageous conversations.
Demonstrate transparency.

Active:
Take a powerful stand for your vision.
Sit down and encourage others to take
the lead.

CO-ACTIVE LEADER BEHIND

Practice generous, openhearted service to others.

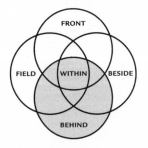

Co:
Foster impeccability.
Find others right.

Active:
Develop your ability to listen deeply.
Acknowledge others authentically.
Be a champion for other people.

CO-ACTIVE LEADER BESIDE

Practice leaning in 100 percent.

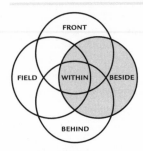

Co:
Design your alliances.

Active:
Focus on alignment rather than agreement.
Use "yes, and . . .".

CO-ACTIVE LEADER IN THE FIELD

Practice letting go of what is known and proven.

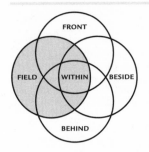

Co:
Trust your natural intuition and instinct.
Be aware of your impact.

Active:
Act without needing to collect evidence.
Speak the truth.

9

The Good Life

The good life. That's what we all want, right? That's what all the fuss is about. It's what parents want for their children. It's what we dream of as teenagers. It's cause for celebration and perhaps a little envy. "Ahhh . . . would you look at that! He (or she) has got it made. Man, that's the life."

But what *is* the good life? What are we longing for? To what do we aspire? There are many who *have* a great deal more than everyone else, but it is not enough. Their homes are larger and their views are more expansive. Their hips are thinner and their faces are lovelier or more handsome. Yet they are unhappy or lonely or restless, dissatisfied and wanting more.

What makes one's life "good"? Of course there are the basics. It's good to live in a country where we can disagree with those in power and say so without fear for our lives. It's a privilege that we have enough to eat, plus leftovers. It's a gift to be healthy and strong. Still, there are plenty of people who have those things and are frustrated and miserable. There are plenty of others who do not and are filled with joy and light.

What's the difference? What makes one person joyful and another unhappy and restless and yearning? We believe the big difference lies in our capacity to give ourselves fully to our world and to receive the richness of experience available in every moment of our lives.

We get so caught up in trying to fix ourselves and others that we miss much of the beauty that washes through every moment of our life. When we can let go of trying to fix things and open ourselves to the wonder and beauty that surround us, we are fulfilled and filled full with light and joy. Our lives become a loop of giving and receiving, of response-ability and responsibility. We share ourselves generously and are open to receive all that life has to offer, the triumphant and the challenging, the darkness and the light.

When we come to understand that we are both creating and being created by our world in every moment, we can engage with whatever comes from a place of gratitude, knowing that all is there to serve us and to grow our consciousness. We can understand that, paradoxically, we are both a full and perfect expression of the mystery of life and a work in progress. We are both the most brilliant expression of life that was ever created and completely insignificant at the same time.

From our perspective, *that's* the good life: receiving and savoring the experience of being human, and also knowing that the expression of our Co-Active Leadership serves a larger purpose that extends far beyond the experience of the moment.

As author and corporate adviser Frederic Laloux says in his beautiful book Reinventing Organizations, "What replaces fear? A capacity to *trust the abundance of life*. All wisdom traditions posit the profound truth that there are two fundamental ways to live life: from fear and scarcity or from trust and abundance."[11]

Paradoxically, as we take responsibility for our world, we are freed from the prison of our ego and its incessant clamoring for approval and the outer trappings of success. Rather than bracing ourselves for the pain that we fear will come, we can open our hearts to whatever experiences life sends our way because we know that whatever comes, we will be all right.

We actively seek to serve the greater good, not because we want to earn approval and love so that we can fill up the hole in our hearts, but because we are so filled full of love and gratitude that it can't help but overflow into contribution, generosity, and service.

What lies at the center of Co-Active Leadership is love. Love for oneself. Love for another. Love for the people in front or behind. Love for the mystery of life. Love for the adventure of it all.

Over the past twenty-plus years, we've experienced working with all kinds of different groups of people, of diverse ages and from diverse cultures. From boardrooms to prisons, from Norway to China, we've experienced the same thing over and over again. Give people half a chance, scratch the surface just a little bit, and you'll find a longing to be intimate, to be connected, and to choose love, as folk singer Kate Wolf sings about in her wonderful song "Give Yourself to Love."[12] One of the things we cherish most about our work is the privilege of watching people fall in love with themselves and each other, and seeing that love expressed in infinite variety.

When fear takes hold, people operate from a very limited version of love, feeling that if they give love away too freely, there won't be enough left over for the people who *really* matter. Our ego convinces us that love is a lot of work and involves lots of action. People need to do something to earn our love. We need to do something to prove that we mean it.

Sometimes people get trapped in working very hard to *get* love, striving and reaching to be lovable enough, worthy enough, deserving enough. It's serious business, this loving thing, and we need to work hard for it and dole it out only where appropriate.

This is complete nonsense. We are all worthy of love, simply because we draw breath. Loving people is actually easier than holding it back. It takes a great deal of effort to stay numb to our interconnectedness. It's quite challenging to pretend that we don't care and that we don't need anyone else. Our hearts are huge and our capacity for love is so vast that it takes a tremendous amount of energy to hold it back. The heart is infinite in its capacity to love.

So the truest expression of Co-Active Leadership is to practice moving beyond our fears and giving in to love over and over in multiple ways, not because it's the right and noble thing to do, but because it is wildly exciting and deliciously alive. We must reach for this responsibility and ownership as much as we are able, forgiving ourselves and others when we fail and continuing to believe that recovery is only a heartbeat and a single choice away.

We are born. We live. We die. It's going to be pretty much the same trajectory for all of us, though it's a shorter ride for some than for others. What makes the difference is the choice to be responsible for our world and to express our leadership in whatever way we are able.

We are in the midst of a huge evolutionary leap in consciousness, what eco-philosopher and author Joanna Macy calls the Great Turning. We are being called to expand our responsibility beyond our own individual survival to the whole of our human community. As we make the choice of responsibility, we work together to cocreate a legacy for future generations of a world that works for everyone, in which the collective talents and abilities of our species are fully realized.

As Co-Active leaders, when we choose to open our hearts and be responsible for our world, we are creating the good life, not only for ourselves but also for all of humanity and for generations to come. We are nourishing the Good Life for all of life on our planet.

It is an extraordinary time to be alive. If we can choose to be responsible for our world in the depth and breadth of our own humanity, what else might we dream?

Notes

1. Arun Gandhi, quoted in Michel W. Potts, "Arun Gandhi Shares the Mahatma's Message," *India–West* 27, no. 13 (February 1, 2002), A34.

2. Patrick Lencioni, *The Advantage: Why Organizational Health Trumps Everything Else in Business* (San Francisco, CA: Jossey-Bass, 2012), 46.

3. David Whyte, "Five Conversations on the Frontiers of Leadership," *Leader to Leader* 2004, no. 33 (Summer 2004), 23.

4. J. R. R. Tolkien, *The Fellowship of the Ring: Being the First Part of the Lord of the Rings* (Boston: Houghton Mifflin, 1988), 345.

5. Norman Vincent Peale, *You Can If You Think You Can* (New York: Fireside, 1992), 91.

6. Derek Sivers, "How to Start a Movement," TED, February 2010, http://www.ted.com/talks/derek_sivers_how_to_start_a_movement?language=en.

7. Don Miguel Ruiz, *The Four Agreements: A Practical Guide to Personal Freedom* (San Rafael, CA: Amber-Allen Publishing, 1997), 27.

8. Antoine de Saint-Exupéry, *The Little Prince* (Collector's Library, 2010; distributed by Macmillan Distribution, Basingstoke, Hampshire, England), 82.

9. Stephen R. Covey, *The 7 Habits of Highly Effective People* (New York: Simon & Schuster, 1989), 101.

10. Laura may have gotten this phrase from Peter Block's book *The Answer to How Is Yes: Acting on What Matters* (Berrett-Koehler Publishers, 2002) but perhaps didn't remember that.

11. Frederic Laloux, *Reinventing Organizations* (Brussels, Belgium: Nelson Parker, 2014), 44.

12. Kate Wolf, "Give Yourself to Love," *The Wind Blows Wild* (Rhino Entertainment Company, 1988).

Acknowledgments

The Co-Active Leadership Model emerged from a network of collaborative, thought-provoking discussions with faculty, staff, and graduates of the Coaches Training Institute (CTI). We'd like to thank everyone involved in these brilliant conversations for your enthusiastic participation, creativity, and support. A special thanks to Jill Schichter, Art Shirk, Paul Byrne, Sam House, Jeff Jacobson, Johan and Gonan Premfors, Kevin French, Sara Lawson, and Heather Strbiak for your generous and thoughtful contributions.

Thank you to our many clients and leadership program graduates for continuing to expand our understanding of what it means to be a Co-Active leader. Being able to witness your growth and transformation is an ongoing source of inspiration and fulfillment.

Deep thanks to the incredible staff at CTI for all that you do to spread our work throughout the world and for being our partners in creating a truly Co-Active organization day by day.

Much gratitude to the Redwoods, our community of practice, for your generosity, love, and support. You are our Co-Active Leaders Within, in Front, Behind, Beside, and in the Field.

Thanks to the amazing team at Berrett-Koehler Publishers. You are the best publishing partners a writer could ever hope for, and it is a joy to work with you. Special thanks to Jeevan Sivasubramaniam for believing in this book, and huge gratitude to Steve Piersanti, our editor, who both championed and challenged us. Steve, *Co-Active Leadership* is an infinitely better book as a result of your persistence, wisdom, and insight.

We'd like to thank Sabrina Roblin, Ken Fracaro, Irene Sitbon, Mike McNair, Josh O'Connor, and Charlotte Ashlock, who reviewed early manuscripts and offered insightful feedback and valuable suggestions.

Thanks to the many teachers who have shaped and inspired us, most particularly WindEagle, RainbowHawk, WhiteEagle, and Brian Swimme. Thanks to the authors whose work continues to inform and inspire us: Otto Scharmer, Ken Wilber, Frederic Laloux, Kevin Cashman, and Lynne Twist.

Thanks to our partner and friend, Laura Whitworth, who died too young in 2007, for being the spark that started it all and the fire that ignited our passion.

We'd like to thank our families for believing in us and loving us. Thank you, Margo House; Jeanny House; Sam House; Heather Diddel; Emily House; Nathaniel House; Alexandra Millar; Helen House; Robert Michalec; Isaiah Farley; Mady Farley; Pat Carrington-House; Connor Carrington-House; Mike, Deigh, and Kelsie Requa; Martha and Dan Fuller; Christin and Stephen Shepherd; Colten Oliver and Chandler Oliver. Gratitude to Carey and Ryan Baker for the joy you bring to our lives and for allowing us to be grandparents. We love you everything.

And finally, we would like to express our gratitude to our global Co-Active community–those who are here now and those to come. You are our vision made real, and we are grateful every day for your partnership in creating a Co-Active world.

Index

About the Authors

For most of their adult lives, Henry and Karen Kimsey-House have been fascinated with people. Their work, both separately and together, has been an interwoven quest to bring people to a greater sense of wholeness, integrity, and fulfillment.

Photo by Phil Saltonstall

Through their background and training in classical theater, their pioneering work in coaching, and their practical experience leading hundreds of leadership programs, they have inspired thousands of people to generate full self-expression, a deep sense of interconnectedness, and an ability to be responsible for their world.

Entering the theater at an early age, Karen and Henry honed their insights into human ontology through classical theatrical training and years of stage, television, and film experience. Henry was a New York actor for 12 years. Karen received her MFA from Temple University in 1983.

In 1992, Henry and Karen met and co-founded the Coaches Training Institute (CTI) along with their partner, Laura Whitworth. In 1995, Karen and Henry fell in love and were married in a three-day celebration in Northern California. The wedding was considered a miracle by both families because everyone had believed that neither

Karen nor Henry would be able to find a partner fierce enough to meet their intensity, creativity, and heart. Fortunately, both families were incorrect.

Today, CTI is a global coaching and leadership development organization offering programs in 18 different countries around the world. More than 50,000 students have taken a CTI program, and more than 6,500 are certified Co-Active Coaches. CTI is fortunate to have hundreds of loyal organizational clients in diverse industry sectors that span the globe, and CTI's faculty of 175-plus members represents a spectrum of different nationalities, cultures, and backgrounds.

Coauthors of the industry best seller *Co-Active Coaching: Changing Business, Transforming Lives*, Henry and Karen are considered pioneers in the coaching profession. Now in its third edition, *Co-Active Coaching* has been translated into 15 languages. *Co-Active Coaching* is considered a seminal text for the coaching profession and is required reading for coach training programs at colleges and universities around the world.

In 1997, Henry and Karen created the Co-Active Leadership Program, a yearlong transformative journey designed to teach people how to be a Co-Active Leader in all areas of their lives. More than 4,000 people have completed the Co-Active Leadership Program and are bringing Co-Active Leadership principles to organizations, governmental agencies, educational settings, nonprofits, coaching clients, and families around the world. The Co-Active Leadership Program has been delivered in the United States, Spain, Japan, China, Israel, Turkey, and Mexico, in English, Japanese, and Spanish.

Today Karen and Henry continue to design CTI's leadership and coaching programs, using their creative insights, bold energy, and instinctual understanding of people to construct unique and powerful learning experiences for CTI's customers and clients.

Henry and Karen live on the Pacific Coast in Northern California with their beloved labradoodle Cosmo(s). The *s* is silent.

For more information and best practices related to Co-Active
Leadership, visit www.coactive.com.

❀ Berrett–Koehler
BK̅ Publishers

Berrett-Koehler is an independent publisher dedicated to an ambitious mission: *connecting people and ideas to create a world that works for all*.

We believe that to truly create a better world, action is needed at all levels—individual, organizational, and societal. At the individual level, our publications help people align their lives with their values and with their aspirations for a better world. At the organizational level, our publications promote progressive leadership and management practices, socially responsible approaches to business, and humane and effective organizations. At the societal level, our publications advance social and economic justice, shared prosperity, sustainability, and new solutions to national and global issues.

A major theme of our publications is "Opening Up New Space." Berrett-Koehler titles challenge conventional thinking, introduce new ideas, and foster positive change. Their common quest is changing the underlying beliefs, mindsets, institutions, and structures that keep generating the same cycles of problems, no matter who our leaders are or what improvement programs we adopt.

We strive to practice what we preach—to operate our publishing company in line with the ideas in our books. At the core of our approach is stewardship, which we define as a deep sense of responsibility to administer the company for the benefit of all of our "stakeholder" groups: authors, customers, employees, investors, service providers, and the communities and environment around us.

We are grateful to the thousands of readers, authors, and other friends of the company who consider themselves to be part of the "BK Community." We hope that you, too, will join us in our mission.

A BK Business Book

This book is part of our BK Business series. BK Business titles pioneer new and progressive leadership and management practices in all types of public, private, and nonprofit organizations. They promote socially responsible approaches to business, innovative organizational change methods, and more humane and effective organizations.

4/18 ④ 8/17

Berrett–Koehler
Publishers

Connecting people and ideas
to create a world that works for all

Dear Reader,

Thank you for picking up this book and joining our worldwide community
of Berrett-Koehler readers. We share ideas that bring positive change into
people's lives, organizations, and society.

To welcome you, we'd like to offer you a free e-book. You can pick from
among twelve of our bestselling books by entering the promotional code
BKP92E here: http://www.bkconnection.com/welcome.

When you claim your free e-book, we'll also send you a copy of our e-news-
letter, the *BK Communiqué*. Although you're free to unsubscribe, there are
many benefits to sticking around. In every issue of our newsletter you'll find

- A free e-book
- Tips from famous authors
- Discounts on spotlight titles
- Hilarious insider publishing news
- A chance to win a prize for answering a riddle

Best of all, our readers tell us, "Your newsletter is the only one I actually
read." So claim your gift today, and please stay in touch!

Sincerely,

Charlotte Ashlock
Steward of the BK Website

Questions? Comments? Contact me at bkcommunity@bkpub.com.

MIX
Paper from
responsible sources
FSC® C002589

Certified

Corporation
bcorporation.net